WIDE of the MARK
Seeking God or Gifts?

Vic Reasoner

3080 Brannon Rd
Nicholasville, KY 40356-9700

ISBN 979-8-9337696-4-6
Library of Congress Control Number:
2026930072

TABLE of CONTENTS

WIDE of the MARK

The Gift of the Holy Spirit

Every true Christian has the Holy Spirit. The Spirit witnesses directly to the believer regarding his or her relationship with God. This personal assurance is part of the gift of the Holy Spirit received in the new birth. It is validated by the indirect witness of a transformed life.

According to Acts 2:38 every true Christian has received the Holy Spirit. In the book of Acts the terms *baptized* (1:5), *come upon* (1:8), *filled* (2:4) and *receiving the gift of the Holy Spirit* (2:38) all refer to the same event — regeneration.

There are two commands in Acts 2:38. The first is for you all (plural) to repent. The second command is for each one of you (singular) who repents to be baptized. There are also two promises, the forgiveness of your (plural) sins and you all (plural) will receive the Holy Spirit. This is the normal order of salvation. John Wesley taught that "every man, in order to believe unto salvation, must receive the Holy Ghost."[1] Yet some holiness exegesis tended to arbitrarily

[1]Wesley, *BE Works*, 11:108.

divide Acts 2:38 into two works of grace.[2] Rob Staples described the attempt to divide Acts 2:38 as "misguided" and "strained."[3] Thomas Oden explained,

> It is not as though one first believes and later the Spirit comes to dwell. Rather, saving faith embraces the indwelling Spirit. Precisely in believing, the Spirit indwells. . . . Though indwelling is not precisely the same as the baptism, sealing, and filling of the Spirit, none of these is detachable from new birth through the Spirit and baptism in the Spirit. . . . The New Testament understands baptism of and by the Spirit as the privilege of all who have faith, all Christians, all who belong to the body of Christ. . . . Baptism by the Spirit is not subsequent to conversion or faith, but intrinsic to it.[4]

Since all believers have the Holy Spirit (Rom 8:9), there is no command in the New Testament for Christians to receive the baptism with the Holy Spirit. Any person who does not have the Spirit of Christ dwelling in him and governing him is "not a Christian; not in a state of salvation," according to Wesley.[5]

Wesley preached a sermon titled "Scriptural Christianity" based on Acts 4:31. At the outset, Wesley noted that the same

---

[2]For examples, see Wood, *Pentecostal Grace*, 33; Hills, *Holiness and Power*, 143-145; Doty, *Lessons in Holiness*, 27; Keen, *Salvation Papers*, chapter 2; McLaughlin, *Acts*, 32.

[3]Staples, *Outward Sign*, 150.

[4]Oden, *Life in the Spirit*, 178, 182.

[5]Wesley, *Notes*, 381.

expression, filled with the Holy Ghost, also occurs in Acts 2. However, Wesley opted to choose his text from Acts 4 because there was no account of any miraculous signs or extraordinary gifts. Wesley emphasized the fruit of the Spirit, rather than the gifts of the Spirit.

However, in his conclusion his standard of Christianity was to be filled with the Spirit.[6] Herbert McGonigle wrote: "Throughout the sermon Wesley gives not the least hint that he thought this fullness of the Spirit something subsequent to justification by faith; indeed he made it very plain that anyone who was not so filled with the Spirit was not a Christian."[7]

In *A Farther Appeal to Men of Reason and Religion,* Wesley used several scriptures relating to the Holy Spirit, including Acts 2, which were in the Anglican homily for Whitsunday. He again emphasized the Spirit in salvation:

> And therefore every man, in order to believe unto salvation, must receive the Holy Ghost. This is essentially necessary to every Christian, not in order to his working miracles, but in order to faith, peace, joy, and love—the ordinary fruits of the Spirit.[8]

In the same tract, Wesley returned to this same theme stating that "every true Christian now receives the Holy Ghost, as the Paraclete or Comforter promised by our Lord. . . . I assert that 'till a man 'receives the Holy Ghost' he is

---

[6]Wesley, "Scriptural Christianity," Sermon #4, ¶1-4; 4.6.

[7]McGonigle, "Pneumatological Nomenclature," 61.

[8]Wesley, *BE Works*, 11:108.

without God in the world."[9]

It is through this baptism with the Spirit that we are added to the body of Christ (1 Cor 12:13; Gal 3:27). Water baptism is an outward sign of the inward work of Spirit baptism (Acts 10:47). When Paul states in Ephesians 4:5 that there is one baptism, it is best to understand that water baptism and Spirit baptism are two parts of that one baptism. John Wesley said, "I never yet baptized a real penitent who was not then baptized with the Holy Ghost." He noted that the "One baptism includes the outward sign and the inward grace."[10]

Spiritual life comes through the indwelling Spirit. There has been an attempt to distinguish between *having* the Spirit and the *indwelling* of the Spirit.[11] Yet the Corinthians were said both to have the Spirit (1 Cor 6:19) and be indwelt by the Spirit (1 Cor 3:16). However, at best they were immature Christians in need of the perfect love described in chapter 13.

Along with spiritual life and deliverance from sin, the Holy Spirit produces assurance. Whoever believes in the Son of God has this testimony in himself (1 John 5:10). Such assurance is the birthright of every believer. Confidence should be the default position of a true Christian. Four times in 1 John the Greek word παῤῥησία (*parrhesia*) occurs.[12] This word *confidence* describes boldness and the absence of fear.

In addition, John uses the verb εἰδέω (*eideo*) sixteen times and the verb γινώσκω (*ginosko*) twenty-four times. In his letter he deals both with objective knowledge and subjec-

---

[9]Wesley, *BE Works*, 11:168, 170.

[10]Wesley, *BE Works*, 28:675.

[11]Wood, *Pentecostal Grace*, 85.

[12]1 John 2:28, 3:21, 4:17, 5:14.

tive assurance. We can be certain about the person and work of Jesus Christ and certain about possessing eternal life through faith in him.

Adam Clarke taught that those who were adopted could know it by no other means than by the Spirit of God. "Remove this from Christianity, and it is a *dead letter*."[13] Clarke said that the Methodists were of the opinion that to be saved from sin meant to be consciously saved.[14] And this direct assurance is corroborated by the indirect witness of a holy life.

In 1 Thessalonians 4:3 Paul says it is God's will that they should keep on abstaining from sexual sins. Thus, they were already partially sanctified and separate from sexual impurity. So were the Corinthians. Paul wrote that some of them *were* involved in sexual sins, "but you were washed, you were sanctified, you were justified" (1 Cor 6:11). This is initial sanctification which comes along with justification. God calls all believers to live such a holy life (1 Thess 4:7). Beyond initial sanctification, God has provided entire sanctification.

In contrast John Walvoord wrote that the baptism of the Holy Spirit is not an experiential but a positional truth.[15] John MacArthur also said the baptism with the Spirit is a fact, not a feeling.[16] Pentecostalism reacts to this rationalism by reducing the Holy Spirit to one particular supernatural sign. They err by teaching a baptism with the Spirit comes *after the* new birth and that this baptism must be verified by speaking in tongues.

---

[13]Clarke, *Commentary*, 6:97.

[14]Clarke, *Works*, 8:259.

[15]Walvoord, *Holy Spirit*, 146.

[16]MacArthur, *Charismatic Chaos*, 189-191.

Yet they claim that the Holy Spirit does not necessarily produce a holy life. Stanley Horton, Assemblies of God scholar admitted, "the baptism in the Holy Spirit is not of itself a sanctifying experience."[17] Donald Gee observed that it seemed possible to exercise a spiritual gift and "yet be out of touch with the Lord."[18] Jimmy Swaggart taught that one does not seek tongues. "One asks for the Holy Spirit, and the tongues will automatically follow." However, Swaggart also conceded, "We do not believe, nor do we teach, that speaking in other tongues will automatically produce a better Christian."[19]

True Christians need not seek the gift of tongues. Rather, we seek to be more holy; more conformed to the image of Christ (Rom 8:29). God will give us the gifts we need for the common good. Don't neglect the gift-giver because of a preoccupation with his gifts. And don't look to the descriptive passages in Acts as the norm. Look instead to instructive passages in Scripture.

Daniel Jennings wrote *The Supernatural Occurrences of John Wesley*. He concluded,

> The Wesley I discovered in my research was a man who fell between dead liberalism which denies all miracles and Charismatic emotionalism which accepts anything that seems miraculous as being real. He was simply a man who believed that God had always worked miracles.

---

[17]Horton, "Pentecostal Perspective," *Sanctification*, 132.

[18]Gee, *Concerning Spiritual Gifts*, 67.

[19]Swaggart, *Is Speaking in Tongues Scriptural?* 37,3.

Jennings documents the fact that Wesley never spoke in tongues nor did he teach that tongues were the evidence of the baptism with the Holy Spirit. In fact, Jennings includes a helpful chapter summarizing Wesley's teaching which equated the baptism with the Spirit with regeneration.[20]

[20]Reasoner, "Review," 11.

The Fruit of the Spirit

In contrast to name-it-and-claim-it "faith," Wesley insisted on evidence — the fruit of the Spirit.

According to Colossians 3:9 the believer has put off the old man with its practices and has put on the new man. And Ephesians 4:24 teaches that the new man is created to be like God in true righteousness and holiness. Here the Greek word ὅσιος (*hosios*) conveys the idea of holiness as devoutness or piety, undefiled by sin, free from wickedness, observing every moral obligation, pure, pious.[21]

Initial sanctification is closely related to regeneration.

> When a person truly believed, he was justified, regenerated, and initially sanctified. Justification is the forgiveness of his sins and his acceptance with God. . . . At the same instant he is born again, renewed, changed from death to life. . . . At that same moment there is a deliverance from sinning, a breaking of the power of sin, and a beginning of holiness or perfection. This last can be properly classified as initial sanctification.[22]

"No one who is born of God will continue to sin, because God's seed remains in him; he cannot go on sinning, because he has been born of God" (1 John 3:9). According to Nathan Bangs the adopted child of God cannot sin because he is entirely separated from sin. "Not that he has not power

---

[21]Thayer, *Greek English Lexicon*, p. 456; Seebass, "Holy," 2:236.

[22]Cox, *Perfection*, 86.

to sin, for he still possesses all the natural moral power he ever did." He might turn away from the holy commandment as easily as Eve and Adam did, but he cannot sin so long as the seed remains in him as a living, active principle and so long as his heavenly Father purges him that he might bring forth more fruit.[23]

Thus, grace is not only exhibited in the forgiveness of sin, but grace is power over sin. Wesley preached,

> Through this faith they are saved from the power of sin as well as from the guilt of it. . . . He that is by faith born of God sinneth not, (1) by any habitual sin, for all habitual sin is sin reigning; but sin cannot reign in any that believeth. Nor, (2), by any wilful sin; for his will, while he abideth in the faith, is utterly set against all sin, and abhorreth it as deadly poison. Nor, (3), by any sinful desire; for he continually desireth the holy and perfect will of God; and any unholy desire he by the grace of God stifleth in the birth. Nor, (4), doth he sin by infirmities, whether in act, word, or thought; for his infirmities have no concurrence of his will; and without this they are not properly sins.[24]

Wesley preached

> An immediate and constant fruit of this faith whereby we are born of God, a fruit which can in no wise be separated from it, no, not for an hour, is

---

[23]Bangs, *Necessity, Nature, and Fruits*, 109-110.

[24]Wesley, "Salvation by Faith," Sermon #1, 2.5-6.

> power over sin: power over outward sin of every kind; over every evil word and work; for whereso-ever the blood of Christ is thus applied it "purgeth the conscience from dead works." And over inward sin; for it "purifieth the heart" from every unholy desire and temper.[25]

He declared that a person "has power both over outward and inward sin, even from the moment he is justified."[26] "By a Christian I mean one who so believes in Christ as that sin hath no more dominion over him."[27] Charles Wesley wrote, "He breaks the power of cancelled sin, he sets the prisoner free."[28]

John Wesley also taught that the newly justified and regenerated soul is initially sanctified and made "so far per-fect as not to commit sin."[29] It is a distortion for Laurence Wood to claim that phrases such as "salvation from sin," "conquerors over sin," "righteousness and true holiness, " "created anew in Christ Jesus," and "the love of God shed abroad in our hearts by the Holy Spirit were common ways of describing entire sanctification for Wesley and early Method-

---

[25]Wesley, "The Marks of the New Birth," Sermon #18, 1.4.

[26]Wesley, "On Sin in Believers," Sermon #13, 2.4.

[27]Wesley, *Letter* to Samuel Wesley, Jr, 30 Oct 1738.

[28]"O for a thousand tongues to sing," (1739) Hymn #1 in *A Collection of Hymns for the use of the People called Methodists* (1780).

[29]Wesley, "Christian Perfection," Sermon #40, 2.20-21; see also 2.2-3, "Those who are born again in the lowest sense, do not 'continue in sin.'"

ists.[30] In contrast, Wesley wrote

> "He that is born of God keepeth himself, and that wicked one toucheth him not? God has "purified his heart by faith," so that his wickedness is departed from him. "Old things are passed away, and all things" in him "are become new." So that his heart is no longer desperately wicked, but renewed "in righteousness and true holiness." Only let it be remembered, that the heart, even of a believer, is not wholly purified when he is justified. Sin is then overcome, but it is not rooted out; it is conquered, but not destroyed."[31]

In John 15:1-17 Jesus taught that those who have trusted in him must remain connected. *Abiding* implies a present tense obedience of faith (v 10). Those who abide in him bear fruit. This fruit of the Spirit is described in Galatians 5:22-23. Summers observed that Galatians 5:22-24 referred to *fruit* not *fruits* to indicate their essential identity, their inseparable connection and harmonious combination.[32] "The fruit of the Spirit are the virtues of Christ."[33] W. H. Poole also observed that the fruit of the Spirit is love:

- Joy is love in action; it is love running over

---

[30]Wood, *Meaning of Pentecost*, 163-165; 209-210.

[31]Wesley, "The Deceitfulness of the Human Heart," Sermon #1 28, 2:5.

[32]Summers, *Treatise on Sanctification*, 49.

[33]Friedrich Schleiermacher, quoted by Dunning in *Grace, Faith, and Holiness*, 427.

- Peace is love resting
- Patience is love suffering
- Kindness is love showing consideration
- Goodness is love at work helping others
- Faithfulness is love believing
- Gentleness is love learning self discipline
- Self-control is love submitting[34]

Those who do not bear the fruit of the Spirit will be cut off from the source of spiritual life. Every Christian is already clean or initially sanctified, but every branch abiding in Christ through saving faith will also be purged so that he will become more fruitful. According to Asbury Lowrey, this purging which results in more fruit is entire sanctification.[35]

> Thus, as a possibility and an obligation, Christian perfection signifies the full cluster and maturity of the specifically Christian graces which give the Christian character its completeness for life and service within the conditions of its earthly environment.[36]

Poole observed that when we are regenerated we experience love, joy, and peace instantly. But the other manifestations require "time and cultivation for their proper development."[37] Thus their love would be completed or fulfilled (v

---

[34]Poole, *Ripe Grapes*. See also the discussion by Sangster, *Pure in Heart*, 100-180.

[35]Lowrey, *Possibilities of Grace,* 251.

[36]Platt, "Perfection," 9:728.

[37]Poole, *Ripe Grapes*, 81

11). Apart from continued faith we can do nothing. But continued faith results in progressive sanctification which produces *much* fruit. "'Much fruit' is the result of this progressive sanctification and growth in grace."[38] The progression is from no fruit to bearing fruit; from fruitfulness to more fruit (v 2); and from more fruit to much fruit (v 5). We bear much fruit by dying (John 12:24) and by abiding (John 15:5).

But this growth in grace is retarded by the remains of sin. While sin no longer reigns in the heart of the born again, it does remain. John Hunt wrote, "Our carnal nature will strive within us, though it does not reign; and it will weaken, interrupt, and perplex us in loving and serving God, though it cannot hinder us."[39]

George Smith explained that a new nature was implanted in the soul when we were born again. This life is maintained in the heart by the indwelling Spirit. But there is one consideration connected with this subject too frequently overlooked — progress in this spiritual life. Yet it is the privilege of ordinary believers to make considerable progress in piety after the attainment of a sense of pardon.

We are commanded to grow in grace (2 Pet 3:18). The apostolic descriptions of spiritual life as little children, young men, and fathers (1 John 2:12-13), as well as the exhortations of Ephesians 4:13-15 and Hebrews 5:12-14, all show that when born again, we ought to go on increasing in grace, knowledge, and holy action, until we attain the measure of the stature of the fulness of Christ.

Smith explained the results of that change when we were born again were perhaps so glorious, that for a season we

---

[38]Turner, *John*, 298.

[39]Hunt, *Letters on Sanctification*, 210.

were not conscious of any indwelling enemy to our peace. "At length, however, roots of bitterness sprang up and trouble us. We became sensible of the existence of pride, anger, unbelief, envy, worldly-mindedness, or other similar evils." While we have power over these corruptions to restrain their action and by looking to Jesus by faith we do not commit sin, yet the existence of these remains of corrupt nature is painful and dangerous. They are sources of pain, as they are felt to be contrary to the will of God by a mind that pants to do his will. They are dangerous because many under their influence have fallen into the snare of the devil. Few have fully escaped being drawn into condemnation under their influence and have consequently had to apply again for pardoning mercy through faith in Jesus Christ. "From these evils, we teach that it is the privilege of all believers to be delivered."[40]

The fruit of the Spirit can increase in quality and quantity. The way to avoid losing ground is to always be gaining ground. In his eloquent way, Fletcher described Christian perfection as

> a spiritual constellation, made up of these gracious stars, perfect repentance, perfect faith, perfect humility, perfect meekness, perfect self denial, perfect resignation, perfect hope, perfect charity for our *visible* enemies, as well as for our *earthly* relations; and, above all, perfect love for our *invisible* God, through the explicit knowledge of our Mediator Jesus Christ. And as this last star is always accompanied by all the others, as Jupiter is by his satellites, we frequently use, as St. John, the phrase "perfect love," instead of the word *perfection*; understanding

---

[40]Smith, *Elements of Divinity*, 298-303.

> by it the pure love of God shed abroad in the hearts of established believers by the Holy Ghost, which is abundantly given them under the fulness of the Christian dispensation.[41]

John Hunt wrote of the maturity of knowledge, of righteousness, of peace, of joy, of hope, of meekness, of patience, of love, and of confidence.[42] Yet John Miley wrote, "The Christian graces of the same person must differ in perfection or strength, whatever the grade of his attainment in holiness. One may excel in one grace; another in another; but none in all."[43]

---

[41]Fletcher, *Works*, 2:492-493.

[42]Hunt *Letters on Sanctification*, 51-114.

[43]Miley, *Systematic Theology*, 2:377.

The Gifts of the Spirit

The Holy Spirit divides his spiritual gifts as he sees fit. The purpose of these gifts is to equip the church corporately. No gift is meant to serve as personal assurance since the Holy Spirit provides both direct and indirect verification of our relationship with God.

Every believer has a spiritual gift (1 Cor 12:7; 1 Pet 4:10). The Greek word for *gift* (χάρισμα - *charisma*) occurs five times in 1 Corinthians 12. These gifts are a synergism of supernatural ability and natural talent awakened by the Holy Spirit.

We are not to seek specific gifts. Rather, we are to seek the filling of the Spirit himself. According to Ephesians 5:18 we are to *keep* filled. This ongoing process is indicated by the present passive imperative verb. This infilling begins with regeneration. Believers are nowhere commanded to be indwelt by the Spirit because they already are indwelt. Believers are nowhere commanded to be baptized with the Spirit because they have been already baptized into the body of Christ. Believers, however, are commanded to *keep on* being filled. While the believer cannot obtain more of the Spirit, the Holy Spirit can get more of the believer.[44]

While 1 Corinthians 12:11 is clear that the Spirit distributes the gifts as he sees fit, in 12:31 we are implored to desire the higher gifts. After considering various interpretations, Donald Gee, a Pentecostal scholar, explained that *love* is the gift we are to desire.[45] Therefore, this imperative intro-

---

[44]Martin, *Wycliffe Bible Commentary*, 1313-1314.

[45]Gee, *NICNT*, 623-625.

duces chapter 13.

However, again in 14:1 we are told to that *we* are to pursue the best gifts. Here, again, we find the tension between divine sovereignty and human responsibility. Should we seek gifts we have not received? According to Gee, Paul is saying that we should eagerly desire the things of the Spirit.[46] This is a sound interpretation.

John MacArthur argued the verb ζηλόω (*zeloo*) in 12:31 and διώκω (*dioko*) in 14:1should be translated as indicative, not imperative.[47] This is possible and the result would be that while the Corinthians were seeking gifts they should have been seeking love.

Even if the subject is spiritual gifts and even if the verb is in the imperative mood, there is certainly no warrant for seeking the lesser gifts and to do so by "helping" the Holy Spirit by starting to babble until he "takes over."

We should certainly hone and develop whatever gifts we receive, but Wesley said that these gifts must be kept "subservient" to love.[48] The gifts are listed in Romans 12:6-8 and 1 Corinthians 12:7-11, 28-31. Peter also describes two gifts in 1 Peter 4:10.

Various scholars come up with slightly different lists based on overlap and whether there are more gifts besides what Scripture lists. Some theologians claim that the Bible also mentions or implies the gifts of celibacy (1 Cor 7:7),

---

[46]Gee, *NICNT*, 655.

[47]MacArthur, *Charismatic Chaos*, 229-230; *1 Corinthians*, 325. Gee acknowledges this possibility as valid [*NICNT*, 624]. However, MacArthur's cessationist views do not necessarily follow.

[48]Wesley, *Notes*, 437.

voluntary poverty (1 Cor 13:3), martyrdom (1 Cor 13:3), hospitality (1 Pet 4:9), music, intercession, and exorcism.

The Charles E. Fuller Institute of Evangelism and Church Growth produced a *Wesley Spiritual Gifts Questionnaire* in 1983 which defined tongues as languages. They also produced the Houts Inventory of Spiritual Gifts from a Baptist perspective, which tested for 16 non-sign gifts. The Wagner Modified Houts Questionnaire was for charismatics. They also produced the Trenton Spiritual Gifts Analysis, designed for liturgical churches. No sign gifts are tested. It includes craftsmanship and music as gifts.

Despite some differences in emphasis, the charismatic movement forced the whole church to reexamine the doctrine of spiritual gifts. The majority position in Christian theology is that all of the gifts of the Spirit are operational. The church still needs them in order to minister holistically. The language in 1 Corinthians 12:7 states that various gifts are given "for the common good." It is too arbitrary to assert that some gifts have ceased, but not all. John Frame declared that he was a "semi-cessationist." He believes miracles, except for tongues and prophecy, continue, but are rare today.[49] This seems like an arbitrary distinction since any gift of the Spirit involves divine enablement which is to some degree supernatural.

However, where the gospel has been established, it might not be as necessary for it to continually need confirmation by signs, wonders, miracles, and gifts of the Holy Spirit (Heb 2:4). While σημεῖον (*semeion*) does not always refer to a miracle, it often designates some notable feature that confirms the truth of the message. Thus, our faith is not in the sign, but

---

[49]Frame, *Doctrine of God*, 262-266.

what the sign sign-ified.[50] The gospel itself is powerful and the greatest miracle is the new birth. Kenneth Kinghorn warned,

> Those with charismania sometimes ignore the biblical teaching that the Holy Spirit apportions his gifts to Christians at his own discretion (1 Cor 12:10-11). These Christians insist on telling God *which* gifts to give them and *when* to do so.[51]

There is also an overlap between spiritual gifts and offices in the church. Ephesians 4:11 lists four offices: apostle, prophet, evangelist, pastor-teacher. These are not merely gifts to people, but gifts of people to equip the church.[52]

The office of apostleship was foundational and apostolic authority is now vested in their writing, the New Testament. Jesus himself was the last prophet, but the gift of prophecy remains. For that matter, Jesus was the last high priest. There will be no succession because he always lives to make intercession for us (Heb 7:25). There is no longer a Levitical priesthood, but the entire church constitutes the priesthood of believers (1 Pet 2:9). Luther declared, "It is true that all Christians are priests, but not all Christians are pastors." For Luther, the priesthood of all believers means that all Christians have unmediated access to Jesus Christ.[53] However, not all Christians fill the office of pastor.

Are there apostles today? According to Scripture, *apos-*

---

[50]Morris, *John*, 610.

[51]Kinghorn, *Fresh Wind of the Spirit*, 113.

[52]Best, *ICC*, 388.

[53]Krey, *RCS*, 8:122.

tles were defined as those who had seen Christ (1 Cor 9:1, 15:8) and did miracles (2 Cor 12:12). They had authority to appoint leadership (Acts 14:23; Titus 1:5) and rule on doctrine (1 Cor 7:12). According to Ephesians 2:20 their role was foundational and thus temporary.

Contemporary "apostolic" churches are therefore forced to redefine apostleship. Those who claim to be "apostolic" usually believe also that revelation is open and do not submit to Scripture as the final authority. In contrast to classic Pentecostal teaching, which holds that the gift of apostleship enables apostles to perform miraculous signs to confirm the gospel, the New Apostolic Reformation holds that present-day apostles have governing authority equal to the original apostles. They not only impart the gifts of the Spirit, they even declare new revelation.

I do not identify personally as "charismatic," but I have no problem with saying that at a corporate level the one, holy, catholic church is apostolic, charismatic, and speaks prophetically. I mean that the church is built upon the foundation of the prophets and apostles, that all of the gifts of the Spirit are operational within the church for the common good, and that the church speaks prophetically confronting everything that is under a deceptive worldview.

The Gift of Tongues

The gift of tongues is known languages. Its purpose is to break through linguistic barriers so that the gospel can be declared to the whole world. Tongues is a sign to the unbeliever and therefore does not function as confirmation to the believer. The gift of tongues is not ecstatic utterances or a private prayer language.

The Greek word for tongues is γλῶσσα (*glossa*). It occurs fifty times in the New Testament. After we exclude the references to a literal tongue or to speaking in general, we are left with the following passages:

Mark 16:17[54]
Acts 2:3, 4, 11; 10:46; 19:6
1 Corinthians 12:10, 28, 30; 13:1, 8; 14:2, 4, 5 (twice), 6, 9, 13, 14, 18, 19, 22, 23, 26, 27, 39
Revelation 5:9; 7:9; 10:11; 11:9; 13:7; 14:6; 17:15

Since the same word occurs in all thirty-three references, our working assumption should be that they all describe the same thing or something closely related. The burden of proof is for those who want to impose different categories on the same word. Craig Keener concluded that Paul's theological emphasis on tongues is quite different from Luke's, but they are both interpreting the same phenomenon. . . . The phrase

---

[54]This reference falls within the textual issue surrounding vv 9-20. See Black, *Perspectives on the Ending of Mark* for the debate. For the purposes of this book, not all textual critics accept these verses as a valid part of Scripture. In their case, this reference would be omitted.

‘other tongues’ probably connotes foreign speech.”[55]

“‘Language’ is the most natural meaning of the word γλῶσσα and best explains how tongues can be differentiated into various kinds (γένη).”[56] Here γένη (*gene*) refers to kinds or categories of languages.

There are a variety of circumstances in the three instances of tongues-speaking in Acts 2, 10, 19, as well as with the Corinth congregation, but in each of these situations authentic languages, not ecstatic utterances, are being described.

Corinth was a major seaport, with two harbors. While Greek was spoken across the Roman empire, as a cosmopolitan hub, Latin, Hebrew, and various Greek dialects: Doric, Attic, Aeolic, and Koine would have been heard in Corinth. Since Corinth had a transient, multilingual population, it was possible that various dialects might be spoken in their congregation. While the people of Corinth were multilingual, McCone argued that they all knew Greek. However, it may not have been their first language. While there is a fair amount of commonality between dialects, some people might be confused and so translation was still needed.[57]

The miraculous gift of languages is either in the speaker, as in Acts, and this is termed *xenololia*, or in the hearer through the gift of interpretation, as in Corinth. The commonality is that legitimate languages are referenced in both instances. A third possibility exists that neither the speaker nor the translator was exercising a supernatural gift. In this case, Paul was giving general instruction that everything done in public worship should be orderly — not merely teaching

---

[55]Keener, *Acts*, 1:813, 821.

[56]Garland, *BECNT*, 584.

[57]McCone, *Culture and Controversy*, 69.

about gifts. Yet for the whole church to be edified, there had to be understanding. Literally, the Greek word is *mind* (νοῦς - *nous*). Christianity does not bypass the intellect, but it should stop with intellectual persuasion. The will and the emotions must also be engaged. While Paul was multilingual, he chose to use a language which was understood.

The seven references in the book of Revelation to *glossa* all refer to the extent of the gospel.[58] The church will be composed of men from every nation (Acts 17:26). Here John expands the extent of God's election from the nation (Israel) to the nations (incorporating non-Jews).

The relevant point here is that *glossa* can only mean known languages in these seven Revelation passages. Languages are also clearly meant in the Acts 2 account, as stated by vv 8-11. However, only locations are cited; not languages. McCone argued that everyone present would have been familiar with Greek, Aramaic, or Latin. For him the amazement did not consist in a cacophony of languages, but the amazement was the report of the wonderful works of God (Acts 2:11).[59] Craig Keener referred to many local dialects in use, "although we need not suppose that representatives of every locality listed here heard languages mutually exclusive of all other localities."[60]

As we work from the more definitive passages to the less clear, *languages* could fit each of the remaining contexts. The word *unknown* which is italicized in the KJV is not in the original Greek. Henry Thayer, in his lexicon of Greek words,

---

[58]This was prophesied seven times in Daniel, as well, in 3:4, 7, 29; 5:19; 6:25, 7:14 (Nebuchadnezzar also uses the phrase in 4:1).

[59]McCone, *Culture and Controversy*, 12-13.

[60]Keener, *Acts*, 1:845.

concluded that *glossa* is languages, not ecstatic utterances unfit to instruct or influence others.[61]

Boyce Blackwelder denied there was any scriptural evidence that anyone under the influence of the Holy Spirit ever spoke in an "unknown tongue." Since *glossa* means language, regardless of the language spoken it would be known to some people.[62] Steadman argued that this gift was the ability to speak foreign languages. He asked, "Who can interpret mere ecstatic ejaculations?"[63] Gibberish cannot be translated.

Pentecost was the reversal of Babel (Gen 11). This theological observation can be traced back at least as early as Augustine. Most who identify themselves as *Pentecostal* do not understand the greatest significance of Pentecost was the establishment of Christ's kingdom. Sam Storms is right — Pentecost was a unique event in history. "There is only one day of Pentecost. . . . The Spirit Himself comes only once. He is now here."[64]

Historically, the modern Pentecostal movement originally thought that they had received real languages and adjusted their theology only after they discovered this was not the case.

In the book of Acts the Holy Spirit was given six times: 2:1-11; 4:31; 8:15-17; 9:17; 10:44-46; 19:6:

• In some instances dramatic phenomena like wind and fire that accompany them; others do not.
• Some speak in tongues and others do not.
• Some are baptized before hand and some are not.

---

[61]Thayer, *Lexicon*, 118.

[62]Blackwelder, "The Glossolalia at Pentecost," 6.

[63]Steadman, "Gift of Tongues," 693-694.

[64]Storms, *The Language of Heaven*, 20, 22.

- Some have hands laid on them and some do not.
- Some have the man of God pray for them and some do not.
- Some have teaching about the Holy Spirit and some do not.
- Some prophesy and some do not.

No two accounts follow the same pattern. Surveying the four major outpourings of the Spirit in Acts, Danny McCain concluded that the baptism of the Holy Spirit in Acts follows no consistent pattern.[65] Of eleven variations, what warrant is there for picking one phenomena and requiring it of all believers? In fact, the normative sequence is stated in Acts 2:38. Some commentators believe that these six descriptions were given because they *varied* from the norm.[66] If that is the case, we must not form our doctrine based on the exceptions.

The quintessential example of how *not* to do inductive Bible study is provided by the following statements:

- Donald Gee acknowledged that there is no indication whatever concerning the outward manifestation of Spirit baptism at Samaria. But he concluded that "we are as much justified in believing it was 'tongues' as in believing it was anything else."He also acknowledged that there is no separate record of Saul receiving the fullness of the Spirit, but he said it is implied as part of the commission given to Ananias in Acts 9:17 Again Gee concluded there is every reason to believe that Paul spoke in tongues because of his testimony in 1 Corinthians

---

[65]McCain, "Baptism of the Holy Spirit," 1-5. See also McCain, *Lord, Lift Me Up!*, 85-86.

[66]For example, Witherington, *Acts*, 154.

14:18.[67] Gee also conceded

> Now the doctrine that speaking with other tongues is the initial evidence of the Baptism of the Holy Spirit rests upon the accumulated evidence of the recorded cases in the book of Acts where this experience is received. Any doctrine on this point must necessarily be confined within these limits for its basis, for the New Testament contains no plain, categorical statement anywhere as to what must be regarded as THE sign.[68]

- While William Durham acknowledged the Scriptures are silent concerning the phenomena in Acts 8:17, yet he wrote "There is not a doubt in our mind, however, that they spoke in tongues."[69] However, an argument from silence convinces no one except those who have already formed their conclusion.

- More recently Larry Hurtado admitted, "The question of what constitutes 'the initial evidence' of a person having received the 'baptism in the Spirit' is not raised in the New Testament." However, he argued that this does not render invalid the doctrine that tongues are the initial physical sign of Spirit baptism, even if we cannot show anywhere that this was the intent of the biblical writer. Experience can fill in the needed evidence where the

[67]Gee, *Speaking in Tongues*, 5.

[68]Gee, *Speaking in Tongues*, 3. This statement was omitted in later editions.

[69]Durham, *Articles by Durham*, 24.

scripture is silent.[70]

- According to 1 Corinthians 12:30, "not all speak with tongues." However, Stanley Horton argued that Paul "is not talking about tongues as the initial evidence of the baptism in the Holy Spirit. The Corinthian believers all had that experience. Paul, in this context, is talking about the gifts of the Spirit and makes clear that not everyone will be used by the Spirit for every spiritual gift in the local assembly." In other words, Horton says not everyone will continue to speak in tongues.[71] Here Horton assumes what he has not proven — that the Bible requires tongues as the initial outward evidence of Spirit baptism. He then reads into the text his own theological distinction. Two pages later he concedes that "no Scripture passage says specifically that tongues is the normative evidence."[72]

Craig Keener offered a better explanation.

> Luke reports such phenomena to assure us that these disciples received the Spirit (especially the dimension of cross-cultural empowerment), and probably not to imply that tongues necessarily must accompany Spirit reception in every individual instance.[73]

---

[70]Hurtado, "Normal, but Not a Norm," 191.

[71]Horton, "Pentecostal Perspective," *Spirit Baptism*, 76. This is also the interpretation of Gee in *Speaking in Tongues*, 7-8.

[72]Horton, "Pentecostal Perspective," *Spirit Baptism*, 78.

[73]Keener, *Acts*, 3:2822-2823.

- While Jack Hayford subscribes to Pentecostal doctrine that tongues is a "sign gift," he "does not think the point can be conclusively proven one way or the other from Scripture."[74]

- Pentecostal theologian Russell Spittler conceded that "the Bible gives no direct answer to this question."[75]

According to 1 Corinthians 14:22 tongues is a sign to the unbeliever, not a sign to the believer that he or she has the Holy Spirit. Therefore, speaking in tongues is not the "initial evidence" for the believer.

However a booklet by the Full Gospel Businessmen's Fellowship asserted that speaking in tongues is a sign of the believer, as well as to the unbeliever. The only proof put forward that tongues is a sign to the believer is the citation of John 7:38-39. It is assumed that the overflowing life described by John is evidenced by tongues, although the scriptural passage never says so.[76]

The purpose of the gift of tongues is evangelistic, not confirmatory. Therefore, tongues are to be interpreted so that everyone will know what has been said (14:31). And tongues are to be used one at a time, at the most three (14:29).

However, some charismatics teach that the Spirit may bypass the stipulations stated in 1 Corinthians 14. Donald Gee did not feel it was necessary to be "under a hard fast bondage"

---

[74]Stafford, "Pentecostal Gold Standard," 28. Ironically, Hayford wrote *The Beauty of Spiritual Language*, a 204-page book which advocates speaking with tongues.

[75]Spittler, "Pentecostal Tradition, Part IV," 4.

[76]Jensen, *Methodists and the Baptism of the Holy Spirit*, 5.

to the stipulation that limited three tongues speakers in any service.[77] Oral Roberts taught that on rare occasions the Holy Spirit moved in a way that was “not in accordance” with the rules he inspired in Scripture.[78] Morton Kelsey explained that “you can tell” when tongues need not be interpreted.[79] Our emphasis should not be to let go and become passive. In such instances we may open ourselves to deception. Oral Roberts denied that the devil can cause speaking in tongues,[80] but this is a naive opinion since ecstatic tongues is regarded as a classic evidence of demon possession.

The *tongues* is 1 Corinthians 14 is the same as in the rest of Scripture — it is languages. This understanding is evident in v 2. The additional *unknown* in the KJV is misleading. In v 14 Paul seems to be saying that the speaker might not understand himself as in an ecstatic utterance, but the problem is actually that the speaker is unable to explain himself and this could be due to emotions too deep to articulate. I have no issue with emotion in worship. I do have problems with affirming — saying *amen* — to what is incoherent.

The key to interpreting this chapter is in v 28 where those speaking in other languages are commanded to remain silent in the congregation unless someone was able to interpret. This protocol presumes real language, not gibberish. Unless the gift in 1 Corinthians 14 was an authentic language, it could not be interpreted. And it also implies that there is no value to the hearer who cannot understand.

However, Pentecostal theology claims that a proper

---

[77]Gee, *Concerning Spiritual Gifts*, 95.

[78]Roberts, *Baptism with the Holy Spirit*, 96.

[79]Kelsey, *Tongues Speaking*, 133.

[80]Roberts, *The Holy Spirit and the Now I*, 56.

recognition must be made between the "initial evidence" which occurs in the book of Acts, and the gift of tongues which occurs in 1 Corinthians. Donald Gee came to this conclusion based on the following unproven assumptions:

- the baptism of the Holy Spirit is a personal experience which in evidenced externally through an outward manifestation.
- the outward manifestation was always tongues. When the phenomenon of speaking in tongues is not specified in Acts it must be assumed.
- when 1 Corinthians 12:30 asks, "Do all speak with tongues?" this is not referring to the "initial evidence," but to the gift.
- all do not receive the gift of tongues but all receive the initial evidence of tongues.
- therefore 1 Corinthians and Acts are describing two different phenomena.[81]

This is a classic illustration of assuming what has not been proven as the basis for the next unproven conclusion.

Kurt Koch warned, "Those who try to gain spiritual gifts, e. g., the gift of tongues by force come into the hands of other spirits. 1 Corinthians 12:11 tells us the Spirit of God gives to those whom He wills."[82]

We cannot redefine *glossa* for Corinth. It was defined in Acts 2. However, the situation in Corinth was that people would speak in their own native language during public worship. Yet these exuberant Christians were incomprehensible

---

[81]Gee, *Speaking in Tongues*, 3-8.

[82]Koch, *Occult ABC*, 209.

to the other worshipers.[83] The real issue Paul addresses is proper decorum in Christian worship.

While 1 Corinthians 14 also describes real languages, and not ecstatic utterances,[84] in this case the languages spoken are unknown to the hearer. Thus, the understanding of the speaker is unfruitful because it does not bear the expected fruit of communicating truth to others. The Greek word used, νοῦς (*nous*), means the mind, understanding, or thought. The utterance is fruitless because the hearers fail to grasp the message. So there is a need for the gift of interpretation.

In Acts 2 the speaker knew what he was saying and the miracle was that the hearer heard in his own language. In 1 Corinthians 14 the speaker knew what he was saying but the hearer did *not* know what was being said. Therefore, translation was necessary. It is possible, however, that there

---

[83]Charles Carter argued that the tongues in 1 Cor 12-14 were also bona fide languages, but many at the church at Corinth had worshiped at the pagan shrines. Therefore, they carried the pagan practice of ecstatic utterances into the church and Paul had to deal with the counterfeit in his Corinthian correspondence ["Gift of Tongues," 56-57]. Harvey Blaney believed the Corinthian believers were lapsing into a pagan ritual, carried away in the ecstasy, unaware of what they were doing. This "unknown" tongue was not a true gift of the Spirit. Paul believed in the true gifts of the Spirit, but not in an unknown tongue. "He recognized that speaking in unknown tongues was practiced in the Corinthian church, but he did not encourage it or accept it was a work of the Spirit [Blaney, "Speaking in Unknown Tongues," 52-60].

[84]In 1 Cor 14 the *New English Bible* uses the phrases *ecstatic utterance*, *language of ecstasy*, *tongues of ecstasy*, *ecstatic speech*, and *ecstatic language* eleven times. The Greek word γλῶσσα (*glossa*) occurs fifteen times and is the same word used in Acts 2 for languages. Thus these translations in the NEB are unwarranted.

was no miracle or supernatural gift at operation either in the speaking or the translation. The gift of languages may be a special aptitude which may be used to advance a spiritual purpose without necessarily being received supernaturally.

In context, 1 Corinthians 12:29 lists speaking in languages and the interpretation of languages as gifts of the Spirit. Paul does not express a concern about the need for gifts in 1 Corinthians 12. Nothing is said about the experience of receiving gifts. Nothing is said about when these gifts are received. Paul does not invite them to seek gifts which they do not have nor does he instruct them how to receive gifts.[85]

Chapter 13 serves as caution that the fruit of the Spirit is superior and is what we should seek. Apparently chapter 14 reverts back to the proper use of spiritual gifts.[86] In this letter Paul addresses about ten questions which were submitted from Corinth. Therefore, he is probably reverting back to this same question. However, the Greek word *charisma* does not occur in chapter 14. Rather, Paul's greater concern is that public worship be properly and orderly.

The bottom line is that the genuine gift of languages and the gift of interpretation work together. Sometimes the gift of languages is supernatural; sometimes the gift of interpretations is miraculous — but they would not both be supernatural. If there is no linguist barrier to be bridged, all that is needed is the anointing of the Spirit for preaching and hearing — which would all occur within the common language. Regardless of how many languages are in operation, in every instance we are talking about real languages.

---

[85]McCone, *Culture and Controversy*, 41.

[86]Thus, 1 Cor 13 is a *sandwiched* in the middle, much like a different argument Paul makes in Romans 6-8 with the alternative *sandwiched* in between.

However, the charismatic interpretation of 1 Corinthians 14:14 is that the spirit of a person prays in an unknown heavenly language that bypasses the understanding of his mind. The charismatic interpretation of 1 Corinthians 14:2 is that *mysteries* are ecstatic speech. Sam Storms calls this the most persuasive argument against tongues being known languages. He argued that this was a way of speaking directly to God.[87]

However, the biblical definition of *mystery* is the open secret of the gospel, including both Jew and Gentile, which was hidden in ages past but now revealed (Eph 3:2-6). Thus, when the tongues speaker speaks mysteries he is proclaiming the gospel in other languages. He is also edified because he understands his own words, but there can be no edification for those who do not understand his language. Since the purpose is to bear fruit, his message must be translated.

According to 1 Corinthians 14:10 tongues had real meaning. Thus, it was real languages — otherwise, according to v 11, they would become *barbarians* to each other. This Greek word is onomatopoetic, meaning that it sounds like what it means — *bar, bar, bar* — and this is unintelligible sound.

While Paul said that he wished all those in Corinth spoke in languages (14:5) and that he spoke in more languages than they did (14:18), he does not make similar statements in any of his other letters. "These two quotations appear to be Paul's way of identifying with the Corinthians before he corrects them" because their practice had gotten out of hand.[88]

However, multi-lingual worship where there is mutual understanding is a foretaste of heaven where believers from

---

[87]Storms, *The Language of Heaven*, 64.

[88]Green, *The Wesley Bible*, 1730.

every language will join in worship. With immigration increasing, the opportunity for evangelism also increases. The church has these gifts of language and interpretation as tools to break down barriers to the growth of Christ's kingdom.

Elsewhere in this book I cite research which indicates that modern cases of xenolalia or the true gift of languages cannot be documented.[89] However, Irene Hanley told how she attempted to share the gospel of Jesus Christ with a Jewish rabbi. As she read Isaiah 53 she said she started in English but finished with words which were strange to her. The rabbi declared that he heard her in "beautiful Hebrew" even though she didn't read Hebrew. While Irene did not know Hebrew, the rabbi claimed "this woman has just driven a knife into my heart." While the rabbi acknowledged the truth of Jesus the Messiah, he decided the cost of following Jesus was too high and he rejected the truth.[90]

I grew up hearing other reports which I cannot document. However, Richard Payne (1926-2014) was a minister in the Church of God (Holiness). Although he was 29 years my senior, I interacted with him in a number of capacities. He also chaired my ordination interview in the same denomination. I heard him tell how he went in the 1940s to preach a revival in Seneca, Missouri. A GI serving in Europe had met a German girl and sent her back to Missouri as a "war bride." She accompanied her in-laws the revival but understood little of what was being said. She detected that they were sincere people and prayed that God would help her understand the message. On the second night she went forward and was saved. On the return trip home she exclaimed to her in-laws,

---

[89]However, see Keener, *Acts*, 1:829.

[90]Hanley, *Israel, O My People!* 53-55.

"I did not know that Rev. Payne knew German." They replied that to their knowledge did not know German. Then she announced that he had preached his entire sermon that night in "flawless high German."[91]

To my knowledge Rev. Payne never had such an experience again. Nor at the time did he even know what was happening. Certainly he did not seek this phenomenon and did not subsequently conduct seminars on how to do it. It just happened. And that does not undermine my theological assumptions. I believe God could do it through me if he chose to do so. I have preached through an interpreter in four different parts of the world. I believe that the giftedness of those interpreters, whether natural or supernatural ability — or a synergistic mix — was the work of the Spirit. I also suspect, in some cases, that they were anointed to declare what I *should* have said and not necessarily verbatim what I was trying to say.

Ecstatic Utterances?

Neither the gift of languages in Acts 2 or the gift of interpretation of languages in 1 Corinthians 14 has anything to do with ecstatic utterances, in which the speaker does not understand the meaning of the sounds he is making. Rather, 1 Corinthians 14:28 declares that the gift of languages is under the control of the speaker — who is not to utilize it without an interpreter.

Ecstatic speech is a pagan practice which is addressed twice in Scripture. Isaiah 8:19 contrasts the mumbling and prattle of mediums with the clear proclamation of God's

---

[91]My memory was verified by Rebecca McClanahan, Payne's oldest daughter, on 5 March 2026.

Word by God's prophets. The Hebrew word for *medium* אוב (*ob*) means one who mumbles or prattles. Their speaking is described as whispering, cooing and chirping like a bird (צפף - *sapap*) and murmuring. Charles Isbell argued that when ecstasy appears in the Hebrew Bible it is to be understood as strange *actions* rather than strange *utterances.*[92]

The second passage is Matthew 6:7 where Jesus tells his disciples that their praying should not be like that of the pagans who babble. This word *babble* is βατταλογέω (*battalogeo*).[93] While *logeo* means to speak or say, the prefix has no meaning. Therefore, Jesus describes pagan praying as saying or repeating *batta* as a meaningless mantra. Nor can true prayer be ecstatic if prayer involves two-way communication.

The prefix "batta" is an onomatopoeia, which means it is a word which imitates a sound. A mantra is a sound symbol of one or more syllables used to induce a mystical state. It must be passed on by the living voice of a guru and cannot be learned any other way. One need not understand the meaning of the mantra; the virtue is in repetition of the sound. According to Hindu teaching it embodies a spirit or deity and the repetition of the mantra calls this spirit to the person repeating it. Thus, the mantra both invites a particular spirit to enter the one using it and also creates a passive state in the mediator which facilitates this fusion of beings.[94]

"Any tracing of tongues phenomenon through church history faces the hazzard of the common lack of clear-cut

---

[92]Isbell, "Ecstatic Utterance, 63; 75.

[93]A related Greek word, *barbaros*, occurs in 1 Cor 14:10 and was discussed on p. 34.

[94]Maharaj, *Escape into the Light*, 204.

distinctions between tongues and prophecy and between the use of foreign languages and ecstatic utterances."[95]

Furthermore, tongues is not distinctly Christian phenomena. Plato mentions it among pagan religions. It was common in the worship of Venus. "Glossolalia is not to be thought confined to Christian groups and offshoots. This emphasizes the fact that the practice is not self-authenticating."[96] Kurt Koch refers to tongues associated with pagan religions.[97]

Tongues-speaking was common among Mother Ann Lee and the Shakers and among Mormons.[98] When their temple was dedicated in Salt Lake City, hundreds of elders all spoke in tongues. Tongues is common among Hindus and Buddhists. In the occult world, spiritualists list tongues as a manifestation of their church.[99] Tongues is considered one of the possible signs of demon possession in the Roman Catholic Church.

Walter Hollenweger observed that speaking in tongues is not even supernatural. In Africa or Mexico speaking in tongues and healings are not considered extraordinary. They can even be found in some indigenous pagan religions.

Donald Burdick knows of no recorded sample of "tongues" which linguists have ever been able to identify as

---

[95]Farrell, "Outburst of Tongues," 5.

[96]Farrell, "Outburst of Tongues," 5.

[97]Koch, *Strife of Tongues*, 32.

[98]Smith, *History of the Church of Jesus Christ of Latter-Day Saints*, Period 1,1:295-297; 322-323; 4:485; 541.

[99]See Behm, γλῶσσα, 1:722-724 for this phenomena in non-Christian religions.

a human language.[100] Eugene A. Nida, internationally known linguist of the American Bible Society, with a team of linguists from twenty-five countries examined recordings of tongues speaking. They concluded that their recordings bore "no resemblance to any actual language which has ever been treated by linguists."[101] Felicitas Goodman discovered this phenomena in a variety of religious settings, but concluded that it is not a language in terms of grammar and syntax. Instead it is a form of ecstatic vocalization marked by certain acoustic patterns.[102] She explains glossolalia as an altered state of consciousness.[103]

William Samarin concluded that glossolalia does not match with a semantic system of language and that it is a "learned behavior."[104] He defined glossolalia as "a meaningless but phonologically structured human utterance believed by the speaker to be a real language but bearing no systematic resemblance to any natural language, living or dead."[105] Samarin believes glossolalia is a learned behavior and does not follow the patterns of normal human language. "A *glossa* is never a natural language."[106]

---

[100]Burdick, *Tongues*, 60.

[101]Edman, "Divine or Devilish" 14.

[102]Goodman, *Speaking in Tongues*, 90-91.

[103]See also Maloney and Lovekin, *Glossolalia*, 8-9.

[104]Samarin, *Tongues of Men and Angels*, 104-109; 199; 231; 235.

[105]Samarin, *Tongues*, 2. See also the summary of this book by Geisler in *Systematic Theology*, 4:666-670; see also Samarin, "Glossolalia as a Vocal Phenomenon," 128-142.

[106]Samarin, *Tongues*, 131.

A prayer language?

Paul states the purpose of the gift of languages is evangelistic. It is not to confirm the baptism with the Holy Spirit for those who have believed on Christ, but it is for unbelievers (14:22). It is not a prayer language. Paul used a third class conditional statement in 1 Corinthians 13:1. He is giving a hypothetical example. He is saying, even if I could speak in angelic languages. However, this possibility is not verification that such language even exists. Daniel Wallace explained that such a hypothesis "offers no comfort for those who view tongues as a heavenly language."[107]

Paul overstates his argument with a hyperbole to make a point. Nowhere else in Scripture is an angelic language mentioned and this verse does not establish that men can or do speak in angelic languages.

According to the Greek syntax Paul was not presently speaking in an angelic language, but even if he was to do so it would profit him nothing if he did not have divine love. Therefore, Paul is not advocating an unknown prayer language, but he is making the point that such a practice would be of no benefit if the prayer did not understand what he was praying. The context is not private devotions, but public worship. Charismatics often argue that the *public* gift of tongues is not given to everyone, but that every Christian may expect the *private* prayer language. Storms devoted ten pages in review of scholars who argue both for and against this position. He concluded, "I am inclined to conclude that it is not necessarily God's will that all Christians speak in

---

[107]Wallace, *Greek Grammar*, 471, 698.

tongues."[108]

According to Romans 8:26, the groans of the Spirit are actually unexpressed groanings which are too deep for words. The Spirit prays through us. Some have taught these groanings were a prayer language, but they are actually unexpressed, wordless groanings which are "too deep for words."[109] John Stott wrote that these groans can hardly be *glossolalia,* since those "tongues" or languages were expressed in words which some could understand and interpret. Here Paul is referring rather to inarticulate groans."[110] We need not pray audibly; God knows the very thoughts and intentions of our heart (Heb 4:12).

Wesley Duewel contended that "praying in the Spirit has no necessary relation to the speaking in tongues." The Holy Spirit leads all children of God (v 14), and this would certainly include helping us pray (v 26). All prayer should be in the Spirit (Eph 6:18). Yet not all have the gift of tongues (1 Cor 12:30). If "praying in the Spirit" means praying in tongues, then only those who have this gift can pray in the Spirit. Morris asked, "Are we to say that only the charismatics have the Spirit's help?"[111] Duewel continues:

> Romans 8:26-27 is not a description of man praying with the gift of tongues; this is a description of God the Holy Spirit praying with such deep yearning that it goes beyond all language. The Holy Spirit uses language when He prays; and when He helps us

---

[108]Storms, *The Language of Heaven*, 187.

[109]Arndt and Gingrich, *Lexicon*, 34.

[110]Stott, *Romans*, 245.

[111]Morris, *PNTC*, 328.

> pray, He guides and anoints our words, but the depth of longing is beyond words. Hence the literal translation is that the Holy Spirit prays with unutterable groanings or sighings. It is not expressible in any language or tongue — but only in a sign or groan. The longings of the Holy Spirit are made known to us through human thoughts and words, but His is the infinite longing of the infinite God. Hence the human words truly but only partially express the depth in the heart of God. The praying soul, while praying with words he understands, sighs and groans with longings even deeper than the words. All true prayer warriors have at times known such deep prayer yearnings and prayer burdens. This has no necessary relation to speaking in tongues.[112]

In 1 Corinthians 14:14 Paul said that *if* he prayed in a tongue his mind does not understand what he is saying. This is another third class conditional statement, like v 1. It is hypothetical. Rather than affirm the practice, he says that will pray in the Spirit but with understanding. How can I be edified if I do not understand what I am saying?

Therefore, praying in the Spirit, as referenced in Ephesians 6:18 and Jude 20, does not refer to the use of tongues and Paul declares that while he will be prompted and led by the Spirit as he prays, he will not bypass his mind.

> Any adoration, thanksgiving, or worship which does not involve comprehendible thoughts and words is not worship of the God of the Bible God is a speaking God. He speaks to man. He wants man to speak

---

[112]Duewel, *The Holy Spirit and Tongues*, 51-52.

> to Him. All worship, communion, and prayer involve understood communication. There is no communication without understanding. Conversely, there is no understanding without communication.[113]

A learned behavior?

Tongues-speaking is more prevalent with those who are submissive, open to suggestion, and dependent on leaders.[114] "As a psychological phenomenon, glossolalia is easy to produce and readily understandable."[115]

> Many people who speak in tongues regularly are aware that it can be quite repetitive. Tongue speakers often have their own sounds and words that they will repeat over and over, sometimes for years.[116]

"Rise upon your feet, speak or make some sound and continue to make sounds of some kind and the Lord will make a tongue or language of it." This was the instruction of Joseph Smith founder of the Mormons.[117]

Laurence Christenson coached, "Quit speaking any language that you know." Resolve to speak "not a syllable of any language you have learned." Pay no attention to how it sounds, for your mind is "unfruitful." As a result, you may

---

[113]Duewel, *The Holy Spirit and Tongues*, 51-53.

[114]Kildahl, *The Psychology of Speaking in Tongues*, 54.

[115]Pattison, "Speaking in Tongues," 2.

[116]Schwab, *Speaking in Tongues*, 46.

[117]Kennedy, *Early Days of Mormonism*, 111.

think that "you are just making it up." Continue to speak in faith.[118]

Arnold Bittlinger admitted that when we lay aside our own language and speak out "the 'risk' is that you will say nothing more than bla-bla-bla," but God will honor our faith.[119]

Nicky Gumbel writes in the training manual for the Alpha Course:

> When praying for people to receive the gift of tongues I have found the greatest barrier is a psychological one — making the first sound. Once the person has made the first sound the rest follows quite naturally. In order to help people get over this barrier I explain this difficulty and suggest they start by copying what I or one of the other pray-ers is saying. Then I start to speak in tongues slowly so that they can follow. Once they have made the first sound they are usually away praying in their own language![120]

While I am willing to receive whatever gifts the Holy Spirit chooses to bestow, I am unwilling to "jump-start" the process. Doing so would result in spiritual confusion and not necessarily evidence anything. The fruit of the Spirit includes self-control. Here ἐγκράτεια (*egkrateia*) describes a mastery or dominion that comes from within oneself, but does come by oneself. Thus, the spirit of prophets are subject to prophets

---

[118]Christenson, *Speaking in Tongues*, 130.

[119]Quoted by Christenson, *Speaking in Tongues*, 127.

[120]Gumbel, *Telling Others*, 182-183. Jacobs, "Crash Course."

(1 Cor 14:32). The participle ὑποτάσσω (*hupotasso*) means to submit or come under authority. The tension here is that the fruit of the Spirit produces restraint while the supposed gift of the Spirit is received by casting off restraint.

"Apostolic" Movements Across History

Writing toward the end of the second century, Irenaeus described the use of spiritual gifts. "In like manner we do also hear many brethren in the church, who possess prophetic gifts, and who through the Spirit speak all kinds of languages and bring to light for the general benefit the hidden things of men, and declare the mysteries of God."[121] The obvious use of the gift of languages was communication and edification. Almost all of the early church fathers, including Origen, Chrysostom, Theodoret, Gregory of Nyssa, and Gregory of Nazianzus understood the gift of tongues, as recorded in Acts to consist of bona fide languages or dialects given for the purpose of evangelization.[122]

Throughout church history there have been movements which emphasized emotionalism and supernatural manifestations of the Spirit. However, Glenn Hinson wrote that glossolalia was uncommon in church history until recent times.[123] Yet D. A. Carson concluded that there is enough evidence that some form of "charismatic" gifts continued sporadically

---

[121]*Irenaeus*, *Against Heresies*, *ANF*, 1:531.

[122]Carter, "Gift of Tongues," 49.

[123]Stagg, Hinson, Oates, *Glossolalia*, 45-62.

across the centuries of church history.[124]

The earliest reference is from Montanus, but his emphasis was not tongues so much as prophecy. Iraneaus mentioned tongues three times: one passage citing Acts 2 without comment, one referring to the ability to speak foreign languages,[125] and a third reference refers to an abuse of spiritual gifts.[126]

Tertullian, as part of the Montanist movement, makes one reference to tongues.[127] Origen makes two statements, one supposing Paul had the gift of speaking the languages of all people and the other disassociating Christianity from the unintelligible words spoken by Montanists. Chrysostom and Augustine were both unfamiliar with tongues speaking and were cessationists, believing the practice had only occurred in very early times and had ceased.

Montanism

Around AD 160 Montanus, a priest of Cybele, was converted to Christianity. He was soon joined by Maximilla and Priscilla, two women who deserted their husbands with the approval of Montanus, to proclaim the true faith. All three claimed their prophecies were God's final word to mankind. They were "spiritual," while the rest of the church was "carnal." Montanus declared himself to be an incarnation of the Holy Spirit, the revealer of "things to come." At his baptism

---

[124]Carson, *Showing the Spirit*, 166.

[125]Iraneaus, *Against Heresies*, 5.6.1, *ANF*, 1:531.

[126]Iraneaus, *Against Heresies*, 1.13.3, *ANF*, 1:334.

[127]Tertullian, *Against Marcion*, 5.8, *ANF*, 3:446-7.

Montanus spoke with tongues.[128] The thesis of Clyde McCone is that "miracle" ecstatic tongues was first claimed by Montanist and that phenomena reset how *tongues* was understood in Scripture.[129]

The followers of Montanus preached the imminent coming of the kingdom of God, when Christ and the New Jerusalem would descent to Phrygia (in present day Turkey). All believers were called to point them there to await the return of Christ. Tertullian championed this cause late in his life, believing its purpose was to restore the church to its purity. However, by this time the original three had died and the movement had moderated. Montanism advocated a strict asceticism, a perfectionistic lifestyle motivated by an apocalyptic expectation of the end of the age and by new prophetic revelations. They also courted martyrdom. It was considered a sign of spirituality to want to die for Christ.

According to W. B. Pope, Montanus taught that the Holy Spirit, as the Paraclete, was not given to the Apostles, but was reserved for a fuller, deeper baptism of the Spirit than Pentecost under Montanus himself.[130]Tertullian claimed, "The Paraclete has revealed greater things through Montanus than

---

[128]Latourette, *A History of Christianity*, 1:128.

[129]McCone, *Culture and Controversy*, 25-27. Thus, McCone (1915-2004), ordained in the Wesleyan Church, takes a more radical position than cessationism. He argues that the gift of languages was never supernatural — therefore it never had a beginning point Scripturally. However, the God-given ability to learn languages still continues to this day. Whether or not his view is accepted, the minimal takeaway is that Scripture is referring to real languages.

[130]Pope, *Compendium*, 3:63.

Christ revealed through the Gospel."[131]

The church condemned Montanus as heretical. Anderson explained that Wesley's adversaries accused Methodism of closely resembling Montanism. Wesley conceded the point in order to refute their argument — that both groups were heretical. In so doing Wesley was functioning as a debater, not a historian.[132] While Wesley was concerned that the same circumstances were at work against Methodism, he made a poor choice in identifying the Montanists as real, scriptural Christians.

There are only scanty references from fifth century through middle ages. This accounts for all the references to tongues through the middle ages. Glossolalia cropped up among the Cévenols in France beginning in 1688,[133] then among the Irvingites.

The Cévenols in France

Charles Wesley had to share a room with one of the French "prophets" who

> fell into violent agitations, and gobbled like a turkey-cock. I was frightened and began exorcising

---

[131]Migne, *Patrologia Latina*, 2:91.

[132]Anderson, *Clement of Alexandria*, 296-298. While John Wesley rejected fanaticism, he inconsistently approved of Montanus in sermon #61, "The Mystery of Iniquity," ¶ 24; "The Wisdom of God's Counsels," sermon #68, ¶ 9; *Journal* 15 Aug 1750, and "The Real Character of Montanus" in *BE Works*, 114:580-584.

[133]see John Wesley's *Letter* to Dr. Conyers Middleton, 4 Jan 1749, 5.3.

> him with "Thou deaf and dumb devil," etc. He soon recovered out of his fit of inspiration. I prayed and went to bed, not half-liking my bed-fellow. I did not sleep very sound with Satan so near me.[134]

John Wesley recorded that on January 28, 1739 several of his friends went with him to a house where they met a woman who was connected with a movement of French Prophets.[135] She went into convulsive motions and spoke a prophetic message. According to Wesley,

> Two or three of our company were much affected and believe she spoke by the Spirit of God. But this was in no wise clear to me. The motion might be either hysterical or artificial. And the same words any person of a good understanding and well versed in the Scriptures might have spoken. But I let the matter alone, knowing this, that "if it be not of God, it will come to ought."[136]

Wesley did not have to wait long to observe the fruit of this movement. On June 22 he called on one who "did run well," until hindered by "some of those called French Prophets." Wesley concluded that these prophets were not sent by God and "earnestly exhorted all that followed after holiness to avoid as fire all who do not speak according 'to the law and the testimony.'"

That same day Wesley spoke to the Methodist society

---

[134]Charles Wesley, *Journal* 11 December 1738.

[135]See Schwartz, *French Prophets*.

[136]Wesley, *Journal*, 28 Jan 1739.

from 1 John 4:1, "Beloved, believe not every spirit, but try the spirits whether they be of God." He told them not to judge the work of the Spirit on the basis of appearances, common report, or by their own inward feelings. "No, nor by any dreams, visions, revelations supposed to be made to their souls, anymore than by their tears or any involuntary effects wrought upon their bodies." Rather, Wesley insisted that everything be subjected to the final authority of Scripture.[137]

In his *Journal* for May 21, 1740 Wesley recorded

> In the evening such a spirit of laughter was among us that many were much offended. . . . One so violently and variously torn of the evil one did I never see before. Sometimes she laughed till almost strangled; then broke out into cursing and blaspheming; then stamped and struggled with incredible strength, so that four or five could scarce hold her. . . . At last she faintly called on Christ to help her. And the violence of her pangs ceased.

Two other women laughed for two days. Wesley recorded that prayer was made for them and that they "were delivered in a moment." He also received a report from Wales that after the preaching was over, they sang over and over with all their might a verse of a hymn "perhaps above thirty, yea, forty times. Meanwhile the bodies of two or three, sometimes ten or twelve, are violently agitated, and they leap up and down, in all manner of postures, frequently for hours together." Wesley concluded that while they were sincere, they had little experience in the ways of God and the devices of Satan. "So he serves himself of their simplicity, in order to wear them

---

[137]Wesley, *Journal*, 2 June 1739.

out and to bring a discredit on the work of God."[138]

Wesley's Evaluation of Other Phenomena

In his *Journal* for November 25, 1759 Wesley observed that God was eminently present in Everton. However, there were no trances, none cried out, none fell down or were convulsed. "Only some trembled exceedingly; a low murmur was heard. And many were refreshed with the 'multitude of peace.'"

Wesley's *Journal* contains a ten-page account of the work of God in and near Everton, evidently written by John Walsh and a four-page report by Elizabeth Blackwell.[139] Revival had come to that area, but it was accompanied by some extreme behavior which included "a strange, involuntary laughter." Walsh "perceived it was from Satan." He reported, "Immediately the Lord rebuked him; that laughter was at an end."

When Wesley arrived some four months later God was still working, but Wesley concluded

> The danger *was* to regard *extraordinary* circumstances too much, such as outcries, convulsions, visions, trances, as if these were *essential* to the inward work, so that it *could not* go on without them. Perhaps the danger *is* to regard them too little, to condemn them altogether, to imagine they had nothing of God in them and were an hindrance to his

---

[138]Wesley, *Journal*, 27 August 1763.

[139]Wesley, *Journal*, 30 May 1759 (Blackwell with an addendum by John Berridge); 29 July 1759 (Walsh); 25 November 1759 (Wesley).

> work. Whereas the truth is: (1) God suddenly and strongly convinced many that they were lost sinners, the *natural* consequence whereof were sudden outcries and strong bodily convulsions. (2) To strengthen and encourage them that believed and to make his work more apparent, he favored several of them with divine dreams, others with trances and visions. (3) I some of these instances, after a time, nature mixed with grace. (4) Satan likewise mimicked *this work of God*, in order to discredit the *whole work*. And yet it is not wise to give up this *part*, any more than to give up the *whole*. At first it was doubtless wholly from God. It is partly so at this day. And he will enable us to discern how far in every case the work is *pure*, and where it *mixes* or *degenerates*.

Wesley finally argued that even if there was a mixture of true and false, "Yet even this should not make us either deny or undervalue the real work of the Spirit. The shadow is no disparagement of the substance, nor the counterfeit of the real diamond." Even if Satan caused people to become proud of their visions, "to slight or censure visions in general would be both irrational and unchristian."

A few observations, however, are in order. First, these manifestations were not sought. Second, there was an attempt made to keep everything decently and in order. Third, there was an emphasis on spiritual discernment and balance. Fourth, these manifestations were present among people who were seeking God for salvation, not among saved people who were seeking deeper manifestations. Fifth, these outpourings produced conviction over sin.[140]

Finally, Wesley recorded his dislike of fanaticism in his *Journal* for April 3, 1786.

> Satan strives to push many of them to extravagance. This appears in several instances. (1) Frequently three or four, yea, ten or twelve, pray aloud all together. (2) Some of them, perhaps many, scream all together as loud as they possibly can. (3) Some of them use improper, yea, indecent expressions in prayer. (4) Several drop down as dead and are stiff as a corpse, but in awhile they start up and cry, Glory! Glory! perhaps twenty times together. Just so did the French Prophets, and very lately the Jumpers in Wales, bring the real work into contempt.[141]

John Wesley taught that we avoid fanaticism, which he called *enthusiasm*.

> Do not hastily ascribe things to God. Do not easily suppose dreams, voices, impressions, visions, or revelation to be from God. They may be from him. They may be from nature. They may be from the devil. Therefore "believe not every spirit, but try the spirits whether they be of God." Try all things by the written Word, and let all bow down before it. You are in danger of enthusiasm every hour, if you depart ever so little from Scripture.[142]

---

[140]Jennings, *Supernatural Occurrences*, 71.

[141]Wesley, *Journal*, 3 April 1786.

[142]Wesley, *BE Works*, 13:112-113.

The Irvingites

Edward Irving was a Presbyterian minister serving in London from 1822-1834. Irving was talented and well educated but perhaps never regenerated. Irving first began to move away from the absolute authority of Scripture, then to a heretical view of Christ, and then to a speculative view of prophecy — expecting the Lord's return in 1835 or 1836.He also became persuaded that the gifts of the Spirit, especially prophecy, tongues, and healing, should occur in the church as a latter-day rain. He taught Spirit baptism as subsequent to regeneration and sanctification, with tongues as the "standing sign." Spoiled by his own success, Irving was eventually dismissed from his congregation, deposed from the ministry, and died at the age of forty-two.[143]

The Catholic Apostolic Church, founded by Irving, also claimed the gifts they received came through the ecclesiastical organization in Ephesians 4:11 which they restored.[144]

After surveying church history, Stanley Burgess concluded that

> while the concept of Spirit baptism was very common throughout the Christian centuries, the modern Pentecostal identification of glossolalia as the 'initial evidence' of such baptism is completely novel until the nineteenth-century Irvingites.

Burgess conceded that in almost two millennia of Christian life and practice, tongues was not associated with the

---

[143]Dallimore, *Forerunner of the Charismatic Movement.*

[144]Steele, *Gospel of the Comforter*, 263.

advent of life in the Spirit.[145]

The Fire Baptized Movement

In 1891 B. H. Irwin, a member of Iowa's Holiness Association, concluded that there was a third blessing called "the baptism with the Holy Ghost and fire." His conclusion was based on a misreading of John Fletcher.[146] Fletcher had suggested that there were many baptisms or outpourings of the Spirit in the Christian life. Holiness teachers often read their own presuppositions into early Methodist literature. For them there was no continual filling of the Holy Spirit, therefore every outpouring of the Spirit had to mean either the blessing of sanctification had been lost and was regained or it was a new work of grace. In the milieu of the holiness movement, Irwin concluded by 1900 that there were six works of grace, adding the baptisms of dynamite, lyddite, and oxidite.[147] He was influenced by Godbey's translation of the Greek word for *power* as "dynamite." According to W. C. Wilson, Godbey was to blame for the introduction of this new doctrine. He said Godbey's translation encouraged people to believe that the incoming of the Holy Spirit is always a spectacular, explosive experience, creating a big noise and a big smoke.[148]

Taking advantage of the discovery or invention in

---

[145]In two chapters Burgess covered "The Ancient and Eastern Churches" and "The Medieval and Modern Western Churches" in *Initial Evidence*, 3-38.

[146]See Fletcher, *Works*, 2:632-633.

[147]Synan, *Holiness-Pentecostal Tradition*, 57.

[148]Wilson, "Well Glory!" 59-60.

> his own lifetime of dynamite, which is derived from the Greek word translated "power" in the text where Jesus promised that with the coming of the Holy Spirit the disciples should receive power, he translated the expression, "You shall receive Dynamite."This has many times encouraged people to believe that the incoming of the Holy Spirit is always a spectacular, explosive experience, creating, as it were, a big noise and a big smoke. One group in Texas actually added several experiences to the baptism of the Holy Spirit. That was to be a separate baptism of fire, then of dynamite, then of lyddite, then of TNT, and so on.

Those receiving "the fire" would often shout, scream, speak in other tongues, fall into trances, or get the jerks.[149] These baptisms of fire, subsequent to entire sanctification were intended for empowerment, special gifting, deeper mystical experiences in heavenly places, and deeper cleansings which delivered from coffee and pork. It also produced new phenomena including "wheel-in-a-wheel" and leaping.[150]

In 1906 Irwin came in contact with the Azusa Street meetings. He abandoned his doctrine of baptisms of fire, dynamite, lyddite, and oxidite, proclaiming that the "tongues" baptism was the one he had been seeking all along. By 1907 a restored Irwin was preaching this new doctrine on the West

---

[149]Synan, *Holiness-Pentecostal Tradition*, 52.

[150]Davidson, *Upon This Rock*, 290; Conn, *Like a Mighty Army*, 39-43.

coast.[151]

Azusa Street

The twentieth century apostolic faith movement based on Azusa Street was an attempt to go back to first-century Christianity. However, they had an inadequate view of first-century Christianity. They tended to emphasize what they thought was important — miracles, signs, and supernatural phenomena. Other restorationist movements have felt that the church needed to adopt a certain mode of water baptism or form of church government. Such movements tend to be reductionistic.

The point of this brief historical survey is that while the American holiness movement claimed to be a return to classic Methodism, it altered Methodist theology through the influence of Charles Finney and Phoebe Palmer. More germane to this discussion is that the holiness movement provided the transition to Pentecostalism.[152] The holiness movement had developed a theological framework of Pentecostalism without tongues. It is significant that two early Pentecostal leaders, William Seymour and A. J. Tomlinson, both attended God's Bible School, which was a significant center of the holiness movement.[153]

Donald Dayton declared, "I find it difficult, if not impossible, to conceive of the rise of modern Pentecostalism with-

---

[151]Synan, *Holiness-Pentecostal Tradition*, 127-128. See also Synan and Woods, *Fire Baptized.*

[152]I trace the historical and doctrinal detail in *Holy Living*, 2:675-732.

[153]Smith, *A Century on the Mount of Blessings*, 112-113.

out the background of the Wesleyan doctrine of 'Christian Perfection' transmuted into the doctrine of 'Pentecostal sanctification.'"[154] The holiness movement had adopted a popular theology that taught believers were not baptized with the Spirit until after conversion.

As late as 1947 Elmer Long was tried by his holiness denomination for teaching all believers have the Holy Spirit. In 1951 A. J. Smith was placed under a gag order for the same teaching. These men, along with Robert L. Brush and Marion Brown, were banned within the conservative holiness movement for teaching what Wesley taught.[155]

Randy Maddox conceded some parallels and precedents in Wesley for later emphases of the Pentecostal and Charismatic movements, but said there are also significant differences. Wesley's distinctive concern was always more on the fruit of the Spirit than on the gifts of the Spirit, particularly more than on the gift of tongues."[156] In a letter to the Lord Bishop of Gloucester, John Wesley explicitly denied having the gift of tongues.[157] The leap from Wesleyan to Pentecostal could only come through the American holiness movement's distortion. Despite historical revisionism, classic Methodism emphasized a supernatural new birth, not a miraculous second or third blessing.

Donald Bloesch recognized that the holiness movement laid the ground for Pentecostalism, "which encouraged seek-

---

[154]Dayton, "Baptism of the Spirit," 122.

[155]Reasoner, *Holy Living*, 2:622-626. These men became the founders of the Fundamental Wesleyan Society. See Long, *Recovering the Wesleyan Emphasis* (2025).

[156]Maddox, *Responsible Grace,* 136.

[157]Wesley, *BE Works*, 11:469.

ing after charismatic endowment in addition to sanctifying grace."[158]

John Walvoord identified the problem in Wesleyan doctrine with those who did not follow accurately the theological guidelines of the originator. To understand that the baptism of the Spirit occurs when a person believes and is born again "would do much to prevent Pentecostal misuse of Wesleyan truth. . . . Had the teachings of John Wesley been followed closely with caution, most of the proper grounds for criticism of Wesleyan theology would have been precluded."[159]

Kenneth Kinghorn concluded,

> Although pentecostalism helped some people, it tended to fall into the same patterns of subjectivism that had characterized the Montanists of the second century and the Waldenses of the twelfth century. Pentecostalism bred schism; and, using proof texts, pentecostal leaders frequently built their teaching on oral traditions, personal experiences, and a strong desire to see outward supernatural manifestations of the Holy Spirit.[160]

The American Pentecostal movement began with Charles F. Parham in 1901. Parham began his ministry as a supply pastor in the Methodist Episcopal Church. Later he came in contact with B. H. Irwin and was influenced by his teaching of a third work of grace. In 1898 he operated Bethel Healing Home in Topeka, Kansas and in 1900 Parham began Bethel

---

[158]Bloesch, *Holy Spirit*, 132,182.

[159]Walvoord, "Augustinian-Dispensational," 56-57.

[160]Kinghorn, *Gifts of the Spirit*, 18.

Bible School. Parham adopted his own Bethel Bible School from Frank W. Sandford's Holy Ghost and Us facility near Durham, Maine.

By December of that year Parham concluded that tongues was the evidence of the baptism of the Holy Ghost. In many holiness groups tongues would have been accepted as *an* evidence of the Spirit, but Parham was apparently the first to demand that there must be *the* evidence of tongues.[161] Parham designated himself as the Projector of the Apostolic Faith Movement. Thus, his emphasis was on experiential primitivism through the restoration of the experience of the apostles. Without grasping the shift in emphasis his wife later wrote, "He preached sanctification as a second definite work of grace, as taught by John Wesley and the early Methodists."[162]

Parham's Apostolic Faith Movement was based upon the beliefs that:

- Tongues was the absolutely indispensable evidence of the baptism with the Holy Spirit.

- The gift of tongues was given for the purpose of world evangelism and would thus hasten the premillennial return of Christ. Tongues were initially believed to be actual foreign languages which would enable this last generation to evangelize the whole world.

This position raises the question of why anyone would need to speak in tongues if he had no intention of traveling to a foreign mission field. Essentially Parham claimed the pur-

---

[161]Parham, *Sermons: Voice Crying*, 38.

[162]Parham, *Life of Parham*, 21.

pose of tongues was to cross linguistic barriers. Wesley raised the same question. "On the other hand, he [God] may see good to give many other gifts, where it is not his will to bestow this [the gift of tongues]. Particularly where it would be of no use; as in a Church where all are of one mind, and all speak the same language."[163]

However, in pentecostal eschatology, tongues were not only a sign to the individual that he had been baptized with the Holy Spirit, but they were also a sign that the last days were here. This was the "latter-day rain."

- Those who received the baptism with the Spirit were sealed for the rapture and constituted the five wise virgins who comprised the bride of Christ and who alone would be taken in the rapture.

This teaching was "borrowed" from the radical holiness teachings of W. B. Godbey and George Watson.[164] The first full-length book to come from the Azusa Street revival was George Taylor's book on the bride, which claimed only pentecostals would make up the bride.[165] Pentecostals claimed that only believers who had experienced the baptism of the Holy Spirit would be taken up in the rapture.[166] Here he distinguished between the apostate Christianity and the church. He distinguished between the church and the bride. Only Pentecostals would comprise the bride of Christ. They were the

---

[163]Wesley, *Letter* to Dr. Conyers Middleton, 4 January 1749, Section 6, ¶ 8.

[164]Godbey, *Church-Bride-Kingdom*, 88-97; Watson, *Bridehood Saints*, 4-7. See also Bloesch, *Holy Spirit*, 202.

[165]Taylor, *Spirit and the Bride*.

[166]Wacker, *Heaven Below*, 253.

144,000 who had come out of the institutional church.[167]

Charles Parham, along with the students, sought the baptism of the Holy Spirit with the evidence of tongues. The first recipient of glossolalia, Agnes Ozman, was unable to speak in English for three days. She even claimed to be able to write Chinese. However, later she rejected the idea that persons who did not speak in tongues were not "baptized in the Holy Spirit."[168]

It was claimed that the students spoke in twenty-one known languages, Chinese being the first. According to Robeck, "Chinese" was among the favorite languages identified by those at Azusa Street. However, they never specified whether it was Mandarin or Cantonese or any other Chinese dialect — it was always just "Chinese."[169]

Parham claimed that reporters brought with them professors of languages, foreigners, government interpreters and they all claimed the students of the college were speaking in the languages of the world.[170] Yet the reporters were actually skeptical. A Chinese man claimed, "Me no understand. Takee to Jap."[171]

It was also claimed that if missionaries would receive this baptism, they could go anywhere and preach the gospel.[172] "Charles Parham originally believed that the gift of tongues

---

[167]Parham, *Sermons: Voice Crying*, 86.

[168]Ozman, "When the Latter Rain First Fell," 2. In this article she stated "tongues was not the only evidence of the Spirit's Baptism."

[169]Robeck, *Azusa Street Mission and Revival*, 237.

[170]Parham, *Life of Parham*, 54-55.

[171]"Queer Faith," 2.

[172]Synan, *Holiness-Pentecostal Tradition*, 92.

would allow Spirit baptized missionaries to preach in foreign countries without learning the native language. Scholars call this xenoglossa. . . . Although there were a few remarkable instances where this also took place on the mission field, for the most part, the gift of tongues was of little xenoglossaic value."[173]

Stanley Horton wrote of three couples who believed they could preach the gospel in foreign lands without having to learn the language, but they were disappointed.[174] Packer wrote that the unanimous opinion of professional linguistic scholars is that glossolalia has no language-character at all.[175] Faupel concluded that "the present practice of glossolalia is not known language. Charismatics and Pentecostals are gradually coming to accept this view."[176] When their early missionaries failed to communicate, however, they had to learn their new language "in the more conventional manner."[177]

In 1914 Charles Shumway made a thorough search for Parham's "professors of languages," but failed to find anyone willing to corroborate his claims. Shumway interviewed Parham at length. A Methodist pastor in Topeka, John T. McFarland, stated that he had been unable to find any outside

---

[173]Martin, *Life of Seymour*, 235-236.

[174]Horton, "Pentecostal Perspective," 52.

[175]Packer, "Charismatic Renewal,"16-17. See also the discussion by Ridgway, "Psychology," 2:916-920; Faupel, "Glossolalia as Foreign Language," 95-109.

[176]Faupel, "Glossolalia," 109.

[177]Synan, "Introduction,"178.

source to verify Parham's claim.[178] Two of Parham's students left and both expressed doubt that the tongues were authentic languages.[179]

Finally in 1925 Charles Parham conceded, "To my knowledge not a single missionary in the foreign field speaks in the tongue of the natives as a gift from God."[180] Later pentecostals claimed the tongues could be those "of men or of angels."What they spoke was not xenolalia, but ecstatic utterances.[181] According to Storms, today xenolalia "happens quite rarely."[182]

After spreading his message through Kansas and Missouri, Parham moved to Houston, Texas in 1905. By the end of 1905 there may have been as many as twenty-five thousand pentecostal believers in Texas.[183] It was here that W. J. Seymour, a Negro evangelist who had previously attended God's Bible School, was taught by Parham. No blacks were allowed in the Topeka school and they were not allowed to mix with the whites in Texas, but Mrs. Parham reported Seymour "was so humble and deeply interested Mr. Parham could not refuse

---

[178]Shumway, "Study of 'The Gift of Tongues,'" 168; 42; 45; 170. Shumway also did a doctoral thesis, "Critical History of Glossolalia."

[179]Goff, *Fields White Unto Harvest*, 79-81.

[180]Parham, "Critical Analysis," 2. See also the evaluation by Godbey, *Spiritualism*, 22-24.

[181]On the failure of xenolalia, see Anderson, *Vision of the Disinherited*, 16-19; 90-92.

[182]Storms, *The Language of Heaven*, 24.

[183]Quebedeaux, *New Charismatics*, 29.

him."[184] Thus, Seymour was allowed to sit in an adjoining room where he heard through an open door.

Seymour stopped by to visit the Pillar of Fire Bible School in Denver on his way to Los Angeles. They believed he was "devil possessed."[185] Seymour took the teaching to an old abandoned African Methodist Church building at 312 Azusa Street in Los Angeles.

Alfred G. Garr was an evangelist with the Metropolitan Church Association, better known as the Burning Bush Movement. Garr closed the Burning Bush Mission and took its members to Azusa Street. In doing so Garr moved from a holiness church which accepted tongues as *an* evidence of the baptism to a pentecostal church which considered tongues as *the* evidence.[186]

On June 14, 1906 Garr became the first white man to speak in tongues at the Azusa Street Mission. Alfred had announced that he had received the Hindustani language of India, while Lillian announced that she could speak Chinese. Convinced that they had spoken in Indian and Chinese dialects, Garr and his wife headed for India as the first missionaries to be sent from Azusa Street. However, when Garr could not be understood in Calcutta, he turned his attention to other missionaries, attempting to promote the merits of speaking in tongues to them.[187]

After arriving in China in 1908, Alfred wrote, "I supposed He would let us talk to the natives of India in their own language, but He did not, and as far as I can see, will not use

---

[184]Parham, *Life of Parham*, 63,137.

[185]White, *Demons and Tongues*, 67.

[186]Kostlevy, "Nor Silver, Nor Gold," 237-244.

[187]Robeck, *Azusa Street Mission and Revival*, 239; 252.

that means by which to convert the heathen . . . . So far I have not seen anyone who is able to preach to the natives in their own tongue with the languages given with the Holy Ghost. Here in Hong Kong, we preach the word to the Chinese through an interpreter."[188]

S. C. Todd was in Macao, China under the Bible Missionary Society. He investigated the work of A. G. and Lillian Garr, T. J. McIntosh, as well as other Apostolic Faith missionaries in China, India, and Japan who had come "expecting to be able to preach to the natives of those countries in their own tongues." By their own admission, he found that in no single instance have they been able to do so.[189]

Yet Todd observed, "At no time has there been any *known* tongue spoken, all has been an *unknown* utterance." Todd concluded that the Apostolic Faith missionaries had been influenced by "a real spirit of evil, personal demons, sweeping down upon God's children, marked as an angel of light — but who comes from the pit."[190]

Seymour came to Los Angeles in 1906 preaching that tongues was the "initial evidence" of the baptism of the Holy Spirit. Phineas Bresee, who was founding the Church of the Nazarene in Los Angeles at the same time, said the meetings "attracted some attention, especially among that class of people who are always seeking for some new thing."Because

---

[188]Garr, "Letter from Garr," 21-22. This British periodical printed a letter from Garr, written from China. While Garr spoke in tongues, it was not the language of Hong Kong. Eventually the translator and other converts spoke in tongues, but it was not English [Robeck, *Azusa Street Mission and Revival*, 256-257].

[189]Todd, "Some Sad Failures," 1-2.

[190]Todd, "Open Letter."

it bordered on fanaticism and heresy, Bresee preferred not to mention the matter.

> But some parties who had the confidence of editors in the East sufficiently to secure the publication of what they have written, have given such marvelous statements of things as occurring in connection with this thing, that for the sake of those at a distance, and the many who are writing us about it, we deem it wise to say a simple word. Locally it is of small account, being insignificant both in numbers and influence. Instead of being the greatest movement of the times, as represented — in Los Angeles, at least — it is of small moment. It has had, and has now, upon the religious life of the city, about as much influence as a pebble thrown into the sea; but what little influence it has had seems to have been mostly harmful, instead of beneficent. It seems not only to have had at least some of the elements of fanaticism, but to be trying to inculcate such erroneous or heretical doctrines as mark it as not of the Spirit of truth. The two principal things which are emphasized, and wherein they claim to differ from others, is, that Christians are sanctified before they receive the baptism with the Holy Ghost, this baptism being a gift of power upon the sanctified life, and that the essential and necessary evidence of the baptism is the gift of speaking with new tongues. As far as has come under our own observation, or that we have seen experted by competent examination, the speaking with tongues has been a no-thing — a jargon, a senseless mumble, without meaning to those who do the mumbling, or to those who hear. Where in a few

instances the speaker or some other one has attempted to interpret, it has usually been a poor mess.

However, things did not go as well when Parham came to preach for Seymour in October of 1906. On August 27, 1906 Seymour wrote asking Parham to come to Los Angeles because "Satan is working." Mrs. Parham said that Seymour continued to write "urgent letters appealing for help as spiritualistic manifestations, hypnotic forces and fleshly contortion as known in the colored Camp Meetings in the south had broken loose in the meeting."[191]

When Parham arrived at Azusa Street in October 1906, he was shocked at the emotional excesses and declared it seemed the hypnotists and spiritualists had taken over. He found things even worse than he anticipated. Parham spoke for the rest of his life of the Azusa Street meeting as a case of "spiritual power prostituted." Mrs. Parham said that Seymour sat helpless.[192] However, when Parham tried to take over, Seymour was "possessed with a spirit of leadership" and sought to prove that Azusa Street Mission was where the baptism of the Holy Spirit first fell. Parham pleaded with Seymour to repent for deceiving the people, to reject the spirit of leadership, and to repent for exalting self or God would humble him.[193] Seymour did not repent or at least did not submit to Parham. Parham was soon invited to leave and he

---

[191]Parham, *Life of Parham*, 155-156.

[192]Parham, *Life of Parham*, 163-164. Parham declared that Azusa Street was animalism [Shumway, "Study of the Gift of Tongues," 178].

[193]Parham, *Life of Parham*, 163-164.

went to the corner of Broadway and Temple to conduct services. Seymour and Parham were never reconciled.[194] Parham warned,

> I have witnessed great dangers in the work here in Los Angeles, and in pointing them out I shall not refer to individuals, but to the work itself as a whole, that we all may see the error of our way and get back to God. . . .
>
> Let me speak plainly with regard to the work as I have found it here. I found hypnotic influences, familiar-spirit influences, spiritualistic influences, mesmeric influences, and all kinds of spells, spasms, falling in trances, etc. All of these things are foreign to and unknown in this movement outside of Los Angeles, except in the places visited by the workers sent out from this city.
>
> A word about the baptism of the Holy Ghost. The speaking in tongues is never brought about by any of the above influences. In all our work the laying on of hands is practiced only occasionally, and then for the space of only a minute or two. No such thing is known among our workers as the suggestion of certain words and sounds, the working of the chin, or the massage of the throat.
>
> Nonsense! The Holy Ghost needs no help! When the recipient of the Holy Ghost comes into proper relations with God the speaking in tongues comes as naturally as any other gift from Him. There is always the real and the false, and anything outside of the operation of the Holy Ghost is counterfeit.

---

[194]Synan, *Holiness-Pentecostal Tradition*, 102-103.

> There are many in Los Angeles who sing, pray and talk wonderfully in other tongues, as the Spirit gives utterance, and there is jabbering here that is not tongues at all. I know that people sometimes fall under the power of God, and that there are times that God thus deals with his creatures that resist Him; but these cases are exceptional and not general. The falling under the power in Los Angeles has, to a large degree, been produced through a hypnotic, mesmeric, magnetic current.
>
> The Holy Ghost does nothing that is unnatural or unseemingly [sic], and any strained exertion of body, mind, or voice is not the work of the Holy Spirit, both of some familiar spirit, or other influence brought to bear upon the subject. . . .
>
> Having guarded this Pentecostal blessing from it's earliest infancy, I feel that it is still my duty to stand against anything and everything that will in any way prove a hindrance to others, or to the advancement of the work. . . . The Holy Ghost never leads us beyond the point of self-control or the control of others, while familiar spirits or fanaticism lead us both beyond self-control and the power to help others.[195]

W. B. Godbey visited in 1909 and was asked to preach. When asked if he had spoken in tongues, he replied that he thanked God that he could say with Paul that he spoke in tongues more than all of them (1 Cor 14:18). He then proceeded to quote in Latin, "Johannes Baptistes tinxit, Petros

---

[195]Parham, *Life of Parham*, 167-170. This letter was originally written from Los Angeles on 1 December 1906.

tinxet et Christus misit suos Apostolos, ut gentes tingerent."[196] The pentecostals claimed Godbey as one of them and wanted to put him "at the front of the movement." Disillusioned, Godbey said he had a language, but they had a demonic counterfeit. He concluded it was the product of "spiritism," calling them "Satan's preachers, jugglers, necromancers, enchanters, magicians, and all sorts of mendicants."[197] Godbey also detected a good deal of "hell-hatched free lovism" in these circles, reporting that gamblers, atheists, whores and thieves also spoke in tongues.[198] The conservative holiness crowd often claimed that the congregation at Azusa Street was made up of backslidden holiness people. In his later years apparently Seymour reverted back to his holiness heritage and taught that love was the evidence of a Holy Spirit baptism.[199]

Cecil M. Robeck, Jr. elaborated on this shift in Seymour's thinking which began about the middle of 1907. Seymour had experienced harshness from Parham, as well as racial prejudice in general. Seymour rejected Parham's doctrine of annihilation and therefore eventually concluded Parham could also be mistaken on tongues as the evidence of

---

[196]The English translation of Godbey's utterance is, "John the Baptist baptized, Peter baptized and Christ sent his apostles to baptize the Gentiles."

[197]Godbey, *Tongues Movement, Satanic*, 5; see also White, *Demons and Tongues*, 121. Godbey also dealt with the tongues "heresy" in *Current Heresies*, 20 and *Try the Spirits*, 8-12.

[198]Godbey, *Tongues Movement, Satanic*, 27-28.

[199]Lewis, "William J. Seymour,'"182. See also Robeck, *Azusa Street Mission and Revival*, 177-178. In the sermons of Seymour, which Larry Martin compiled from 1907-1908, there was a greater emphasis on tongues [Martin, *Azusa Street Sermons*].

baptism in the Holy Spirit. Within six months of Parham's arrest, Seymour declared that divine love was the real evidence that a person had received the baptism with the Holy Ghost. Ultimately Seymour's position on Parham's initial evidence "had hardened into a clear rejection." By 1915 Seymour wrote, "Some people to-day cannot believe that they have the Holy Ghost without some outward signs." Seymour declared, "that is Heathenism."[200]

In his *Doctrines and Discipline of the Asuza Street Apostolic Faith Mission*, Seymour the founder and general overseer declared, "Wherever the doctrine of the Baptism in the Holy Spirit will only be known as the evidence of speaking in tongues, that work will be an open door for witches and spiritualists, and free loveism." Later in the same work, Article V was amended to read, "The speaking in tongues being one of the 'signs following' the baptised believers and other evidence of the Bible casting out devils, healing the sick and with the fruits of spirit accompanying the signs."

The Charismatic Renewal

The charismatic movement began in 1960 when Dennis Bennett, rector of St. Mark's Episcopal Church in Van Nuys, California, spoke in tongues and introduced the experience to his congregation.[201] Charismatics may be Protestant or Catholic, Reformed or Wesleyan, Trinitarian or even Unitarian-Universalist.[202] The charismatic experience of speaking in tongues unites people through a common experience who

---

[200]Robeck, "William J. Seymour,'" 80-89; Seymour, *Doctrines*, 8.

[201]Williams, "Charismatic Movement," 205.

[202]Quebedeaux, *New Charismatics*, 127.

could not agree theologically. In spite of the diversity within the movement, it is united by a common experience: the baptism of the Holy Spirit with accompanying gifts.[203]

Bennett taught that every Christian is indwelt by the Holy Spirit, "but he or she still needs to speak in tongues. . . . It is not an optional 'gift' among many." "You start speaking in tongues the same way you start speaking any language, by beginning to make sounds." He taught two ways that tongues were used, as a prayer language and the gift of tongues. The prayer language does not need interpretation, but the less common practice of public speaking in tongues does require interpretation. "With the prayer language you can speak in tongues any time you decide to do so, but you do not just decide you'd like to bring a gift of tongues." Yet he cautioned, "Speaking in the Spirit doesn't show how holy you are and you don't do it to prove you have the Holy Spirit living in you."[204] Bennett actually connected childish babbling with glossolalia and claimed "it is not unusual to find a person who has been speaking in tongues ever since childhood but who did not know the significance of what he or she was doing.[205] Tongues then becomes a non-rational experience or a "leap in the dark." Without necessarily understanding existential philosophy, it is common for pentecostal preachers to exhort their congregation to quit trying to understand with their minds and "just let go." But how can the will surrender to what the intellect cannot grasp? Paul asked, How can we say "amen" to what we do not understand? (1 Cor 14:16).

---

[203]Quebedeaux, *New Charismatics*, 5.

[204]Bennett, *How to Pray*, 75; 54; 18; 27; 56.

[205]Bennett, "The Gifts of the Holy Spirit," 26.

The charismatic movement did not produce a systematic theology for over thirty years.[206] Experience becomes all important, yet without the absolute truth of Scripture experience can mean anything. Yet their emphasis on the Holy Spirit forced all the denominations influenced by charismatics to develop or redefine the role of the Holy Spirit. While the early church held councils to state the ecumenical doctrines concerning the Father and the Son, no such council has ever been held to deal with the doctrines of the Spirit. While not every answer they suggested can be accepted as adequate, the charismatics can at least be thanked for forcing the question.

However, we must distinguish between the general term *charismatic* and the specific historical *charismatic* movement. In a general sense W. T. Purkiser is right, "In the New Testament use of the term, all Christians are charismatic."[207] Fellow Nazarene Rob Staples also declared that we believe in spiritual gifts." Thus we, too, are charismatics. But we are charismatics *who do not speak in unknown tongues.*"[208]

However, Howard Snyder saw this "openness to the gifts of the Spirit" as evidence that Wesley was charismatic.[209] Never mind everything Wesley said to the contrary, Snyder claims that John Wesley's theology is charismatic and Methodism was a charismatic movement. His chapter, "The Charismatic Wesley," uses *charismatic* in the general sense

---

[206]Farah, "America's Pentecostals," 24-25. J. Rodman Williams completed his *Renewal Theology*, a systematic theology from a charismatic perspective, in 1992. The three volumes were reprinted in one volume by Zondervan in 1996.

[207]Purkiser, *The Gifts of the Spirit*, 17.

[208]Staples, "A Rose is a Rose," 25.

[209]Snyder and Runyan, *Divided Flame*, 57.

to prove that Wesley was *charismatic* in the specific sense.[210] He does not think Wesley would have "necessarily opposed the modern phenomenon of glossolalia." He says the pentecostals and charismatics are here to stay and that the holiness bodies are "softening their opposition" and taking a second look.[211] Snyder's conclusion is that "tongues-speaking is legitimate whenever it is prompted by the Holy Spirit, regardless of one's theology!"[212]

The Third Wave

Peter Wagner coined the term "third wave" in 1983 to refer to a third wave of pentecostalism with Azusa Street representing the first wave and the charismatic movement representing the second wave. Wagner did not consider himself to be pentecostal or charismatic, but had been teaching a class on signs and wonders at Fuller Theological Seminary.[213]

---

[210]Thus, "Wesley's theology is charismatic in its stress on God's grace in the life and experience of the church." Secondly, Snyder asserts, "Wesley's understand of the church and Christian experience can be understood as charismatic because of the place of the Holy Spirit in his theology and because of his openness to the gifts of the Spirit." Furthermore, "Wesley's theology is charismatic in its emphasis on the church as community." And finally, "Wesley's theology is charismatic in its tension with institutional expressions of the church" [*The Divided Flame*, 54-64].

[211]Snyder, "Church as Holy and Charismatic," 16,22.

[212]Snyder and Runyan, *Divided Flame*, 21.

[213]Wagner, "Signs, Wonders and Church Growth,"42-49. See also Chandler, "Fuller Seminary,"48-49; Patterson, "Cause for

Ironically, a survey by Gallup Poll indicated that 19% of all adult Americans (29 million) consider themselves to be Pentecostal or charismatic, yet only 17% of these people (5 million or 4% of the general population) have spoken in tongues.[214] More recently, the Pew forum on Religion and Public Life found that 49% of all Pentecostals and 32% of all Charismatics never speak in tongues.[215]

Those within the third wave are evangelicals who exercise the gifts of the Spirit without accepting the previous labels. They see the work of the Holy Spirit in divine healing, new prophecies, and casting out of demons. However, they deny any "second blessing," instead teaching that believers are baptized with the Spirit at the time of their conversion.[216]

John Wimber declared that conversion and Holy Spirit baptism are simultaneous experiences."How can we experience Spirit baptism? It comes at conversion."[217] They do not

---

Concern," 20, both of which reported the course had been cancelled due to problems.

[214]Kantzer, "Charismatics Among Us,"25. Olsen cited an October 2006 survey by Pew Forum on Religion and Public Life which revealed that at least 40% of Pentecostals in six of the ten countries surveyed said they had never prayed or spoken in tongues. Only half of U. S. Pentecostals had spoken in tongues [Olsen, "What Really Unites Pentecostals?"18]. According to statistics in the *New International Dictionary of Pentecostal and Charismatic Movements* only 5%-35% of all Pentecostals had spoken in tongues, either initially or on an ongoing basis [Barrett and Johnson, "Global Statistics," 291].

[215]McMullen, "Holding Their Tongues," 16.

[216]Storms, *The Language of Heaven*, 42-43.

[217]Wimber, *Power Points*, 136.

always insist on glossolalia.[218]

The Vineyard movement, led by John Wimber, emphasized healing and deliverance, connecting this with power evangelism.[219] "For Wimber, the heart of the Christian faith resides in an experience of the power and love of God, not in a creed."[220] Wimber emphasized a paradigm shift away from biblical doctrine toward experience.[221] Wimber emphasized that God is bigger than His Word. "All that is in the Bible is true, but not all truth is in the Bible. We integrate all truth, both biblical and other, into our experience of living."[222]

For Wimber the power of God lies in activity — signs, wonders, healings, miracles, church growth. Thus, the third wave emphasizes evangelism through signs and wonders. The Vineyard movement taught multiple fillings of the Holy Spirit and did not understand tongues to be the "initial evidence." The emphasis was on empowerment by the Holy Spirit. This empowerment was demonstrated through the charismatic gifts of prophecy and healing more than speaking in tongues. Yet Grant Wacker call it "runaway pragmatism," because "the usefulness of signs and wonders is so raw, so unvarnished, one can scarcely tell where pragmatism ends and manipulation begins."[223] According to Jesus, it is possible to prophesy, cast out demons, and do mighty works without being genuine Christians (Matt 7:22-23). We should rejoice that our names

---

[218]Pawson, "Mixed Blessing," 84.

[219]Stafford, "Testing the Wine," 17-22.

[220]Percy, *Words, Wonders and Power*, 83.

[221]Wagner, *Acts of the Holy Spirit*, 123.

[222]Goodwin, "Testing the Fruit of the Vineyard."

[223]Wacker, "Wimber and Wonders," 18.

are written in heaven (Luke 10:20).

Apologists for the extraordinary phenomena within the "third wave" have sometimes appealed to the precedent of the "jerks" or religious exercises associated with the Cane Ridge Camp Meeting in 1801. Peter Cartwright described these manifestations and concluded that the jerks were either a judgment sent from God to bring sinners to repentance or to show professors that God could work sovereignly. Cartwright was sure that there was a great deal of "copy-cat" manifestations, but for others it was perfectly involuntary. However, unlike the more modern variation in which manifestations are sought and encouraged, in those days prayer was advocated as a remedy for the jerks. Concerning the "running, jumping, barking exercise," Cartwright reported, "The Methodist preachers generally preached against this extravagant wildness."[224]

Based on a continutionist view that the gift of prophecy is for today, they redefine it as fallible and not the same as what was recorded in Scripture. According to Oropeza another of the Kansas City "prophets" achieved no more than a 65% success rate in the fulfillment of his prophecies.[225] Sam Storm explained that prophecy is "occasionally fallible," although God is infallible, because we misperceive, misinterpret, and misapply it.[226]

Thankfully, we have a more sure word of prophecy — not *less* sure. According to 2 Peter 1:20-21 the prophets of old were carried along by the Spirit of God as wind in the sails moves a boat along the water.

---

[224]Cartwright, *Autobiography*, 45-46.

[225]Oropeza, *Time to Laugh*, 56.

[226]Storm, "A Third Wave View," 207-208.

> Above all, you must understand that no prophecy of Scripture came about by the prophet's own interpretation. For prophecy never had its origin in the will of man, but men spoke from God as they were carried along by the Holy Spirit.

However, Scripture can also be misinterpreted and misapplied. Therefore, we must rightly handle the Word of truth (2 Tim 2:15). The real issue is whether contemporary prophecies are equal to new Scripture and an open canon. If any new prophecy must be tested by Scripture (1 John 4:1), it cannot be equal with Scripture. Yet if their new revelations are actually God's words, how can they not be as authoritative as Scripture? Wayne Grudem's answer is that the prophets in the New Testament did not have the same authority as prophets in the Old Testament. So, while he believes that prophecy continues even in our day, he does not demand that contemporary "prophecy" conform to the mandate of Deuteronomy 18:20-22.[227]

In his book *The Rise and Fall of the Kansas City Prophets* (2026), Sam Storms warned against prioritizing spiritual gifts over character. However, this is a both-and issue, not an either-or dilemma. The classic Methodist position accepts the validity of spiritual gifts, but puts the emphasis on spiritual fruit.

However, classic Methodism contended for the direct witness of the Spirit. According to Wesley,

> The testimony of the Spirit is an inward impression on the soul, whereby the Spirit of God directly "witnesses to my spirit that I am a child of God"; that

[227]Grudem, *Systematic Theology*, 1049-1061.

> Jesus Christ hath loved me, and given himself for me; that all my sins are blotted, out, and I, even I, am reconciled to God.[228]

While such assurance is taught in Scripture, this assurance is directly given to the believer — not indirectly through Scripture alone. This revelation does not impart new doctrine, but it is direct communication. God gives personal guidance but not new revelation.

Since the verb *witness* is present tense in Romans 8:16, he continues to speak to his own. We affirm that God still speaks, but that he does not contradict what he has already said. Thus, Methodism also taught an indirect witness which corroborates the direct witness. This indirect witness is the fruit of the Spirit.

David Pawson expressed hope that there would be a *fourth wave*, in which the Word and the Spirit would be integrated as they were in the New Testament. Call it what you will, I would express openness to such possibilities. At a most basic level, people are hungry for the presence of God. However Pawson continued, "Now I fear that Word and Spirit are drifting apart again, with some seeking the Spirit but less interested in Scripture."[229]

The New Apostolic Reformation

This movement arose in the 1990s, based on the theology

---

[228]Wesley, "Witness of the Spirit, I," Sermon #10, 1.7.

[229]Pawson, "Mixed Blessing," 87.

of C. Peter Wagner. The Bethel Church in Redding, California is a visible face to the apostolic network. In addition to the traditional Pentecostal emphases, the added emphasis is that spiritual gifts come through these modern apostles and prophets. In order to receive the gift, one must first submit to their authority. Pastor Bill Johnson believes that a return to the five-fold offices stated in Ephesians 4:11 will facilitate the end-time revival. Johnson probably does not even know that Edward Irving taught the same thing.

Signs, wonders, and miracles are supposed to come through these modern apostles and prophets. Evangelists and teachers are not emphasized so much; the emphasis is on restoring the missing apostles and prophets in this hierarchy. And for $425 per person aspiring prophets can accelerate their prophetic calling by enrolling in Bethel's annual conferences.

But the Ephesians passage does not actually teach a hierarchy. Exegetically, there is difference of opinion as to whether these are offices or gifts. Everyone who refers to the "fivefold ministry" is not necessarily espousing the same concept. Furthermore, there is also the question of whether the passage lists four or five, since pastor-teacher is stated with the Greek connecting particle και (*kai*).

I hold the position that the offices of apostle and prophet have ceased, unlike gifts which have not ceased. If this is correct, 1 Corinthians 12:27-31 mixes offices and gifts. If so, Paul is giving almost a random sampling of structure within the church. Granted, *first*, *second*, *third* could denote a hierarchy. If this is the case, the germane point for this discussion is that the gift of tongues is clearly designated as the least. And Paul clearly states that all do not speak in tongues.

But it is not mandatary in my overarching evaluation whether apostle and prophet are designated as offices or gifts. Germain to this discussion, the NAR places a significant emphasis on speaking in tongues. This practice is considered a key "sign and wonder" that validates the movement's claim to restore the church to its original power and the active presence of apostolic gifts in the modern era.

The Theology of Speaking in Tongues

Theology is relatively unimportant to charismatics. Larry Hart explained, "Strictly speaking, Spirit baptism is a metaphor, not a doctrine. Further, it is a metaphor whose usage is clearly not univocal within the New Testament." Hart argued that in the New Testament Spirit baptism refers to the eschatological redemptive work of Jesus, Christian initiation, the Christian life, and empowerment for Christian mission and ministry. He concluded, "There is no one 'Charismatic position' on spirit baptism."[230]Many charismatics have come to believe that being filled with the Spirit is an experience which begins with justification and continues one's whole lifetime. For them Spirit-baptism is not one but many gifts, not two but many experiences.[231]

The modern "Pentecostal" movement has never agreed as to what speaking in tongues actually signified. It is an experience not a doctrine — although the purpose of spiritual gifts is clearly stated in Scripture. What happened at Azusa Street has undergone a major historical revision. What was once scorned is now sought. The phenomena of glossolalia has been redefined from xenolalia, to ecstatic utterances, the language of angels, or a prayer language.

While the Azusa Street "revival" is popularly touted as the last-days revival, the phenomena of speaking in tongues had various doctrinal interpretations. First, tongues was the catalyst to facility the great end-time world revival. Then it was the initial confirmation of a third work of grace for those with a holiness background. One must be saved first and that

---

[230]Hart, "Charismatic Perspective," 108-109.

[231]Tuttle, "Guidelines," 7.

was forgiveness. One must be sanctified secondly, and that was to prepare a clean vessel for the baptism with the Holy Spirit, which was the third blessing. Those without a holiness framework reduced the order of salvation to a two-step paradigm: first forgiveness and then Spirit baptism.

Unitarian Pentecostals, who rejected the Trinity, held that speaking in tongues accompanied the new birth.[232] However, it seems that getting the experience was always more important than knowing what it signified. Thus, the three main branches of Pentecostalism became organized, then institutionalized. The one emphasis they held in common is that they were the only sect of Christianity that was right and that nominal Christians needed to "come out" of dead, worldly churches and affiliate with them.

Among Roman Catholics the charismatic movement has produced a new devotion to the virgin Mary and the Mass.[233]

However, third-world Pentecostals focus on corporate worship, singing together, and Christian education, not tongues.[234] Thus, the important consideration is not to quibble over labels and categories. What is significant in my argument is that the gift of tongues has a purpose and should not be relegated simply to an experience.

I used to feel that the rhetorical question in James 3:11 amounted to a wholesale condemnation of the pentecostal movement. Bitter water and fresh water cannot come from the same source. The historical roots of pentecostalism were sufficiently corrupt to condemn the entire movement. However, I have met too many good pentecostal pastors who were

---

[232]Hall, "Oneness Pentecostal,"184.

[233]O'Connor, *Pentecostal in the Catholic Church*, 15.

[234]Hollenweger, "Pentecostalism's Global Language," 42.

helping their congregations find a spiritual balance and had genuine saints in their congregation. In some instances people were attracted to pentecostalism because they were sick of the dead formality of the mainline denominations. And in many instances, those who identify themselves as pentecostal or charismatic have not even spoken in tongues. They simply believe in the gifts of the Spirit. And Pentecostalism must be given credit for breaking the mindset of Western rationalism and making a supernatural worldview legitimate.

Thus, I have generally avoided the *ad hominem* logical fallacy, which means that I dismiss the doctrine by pointing to character defects in those who advocate tongues-speaking. However, Jesus taught that we could recognize false prophets by their fruits (Matt 7:20). Bad teaching will eventually produce unholy living.

Clark Pinnock explained that the baptism in the Spirit, for charismatics, does not refer to a doctrine to be believed, but it is an encounter which must be experienced.[235] He also argued that the gift of tongues must be evaluated Scripturally and not on the basis of experience. It can be harmful for a Christian to seek a gift which the Scriptures do not explicitly promise. Nowhere are we commanded either to be baptized with the Spirit or to seek the gift of tongues. "The reason why Paul did not ask the Corinthian Christians to be baptized with the Spirit is simple: they had already been baptized with him (1 Cor 12:13)." We must formulate our doctrine from the epistles, not the historical account of Acts.[236] Along with Grant Osborne, Pinnock wrote, "The Book of Acts shows, that

[235]Pinnock, *Evangelical Theology*, 1-9.

[236]Pinnock, "Tongues," 128-141.

tongues was never sought in the apostolic age."[237]

However, Pinnock is disappointing in his later book *Flame of Love* which reflects both his open theism and his departure from a previously held view on biblical inerrancy. He also advocates speaking in unknown tongues. He even said that with the Spirit's help, one "may need to go beyond Scripture in carrying out its intentions." For Pinnock "revelation has not ceased." He explained that there is shallowness in the rhetoric of "Scripture only" and said that over the years he had come to realize "how Wesleyan my moves in method and theism were."[238] But this move away from the authority of Scripture to a subjective experientialism is a distortion of Wesley.

---

[237]Pinnock, "Truce Proposal for the Tongues Controversy," 6-9.

[238]Pinnock, "Evangelical Theologians," 12.

My Journey

You may choose to skip this section, but I am making a connecting point at the end. In 1961 I contracted spinal meningitis. Some accounts said I would die; other accounts that I would be paralyzed for life. However, my grandpa and pastor prayed for my healing. I did not "claim" healing myself since I was in a coma. They did not command God nor "declare" that I was healing. Instead, as they prayed that God would reveal his will, they were given the gift of faith. The next day I regained consciousness and word went through the hospital that a miracle had occurred.[239]

As a teenager I came under the convicting work of the Spirit that I needed more that I had. I started seeking God in July 1972. I had heard about speaking in tongues and opened myself to that possibility. I had also heard that sometimes you have to "jump start" the process, but I was unwilling to do so because I might never know if it was truly from God or simply "worked up." In those times of seeking I was always reminded to hurtful things that I had done and said. I was in a process making apologies and restitution when I went to a camp meeting, actually riding with the evangelist. I asked him everything I could think up about the phenomenon in the book of Acts — especially the fact that it was never completely consistent. He gave me some pat answers but I didn't think he really knew himself.

On Monday, August 7, I went forward and declared that I wanted the baptism with the Holy Spirit. For some reason I fully expected an electrical jolt. Instead, the Holy Spirit dealt with me about surrender. I became willing to never marry,

---

[239]Yocum, *Conformed to Christ*, 134-136; Yocum, "Five-year-old Victor Walks Again," 9.

although I never felt that was a requirement, rather it was willingness that God wanted. I was married in 1976. I also agreed to preach if I was ever called. That call came on January 10, 1975 and while I did not expect it, I shook under the power of God.

From my healing in 1961 until I went forward in 1972 saints of God frequently told me that God had something special for me to do. When I testified in 1975 that I was called into ministry, it seemed that I was the last to know it! It was 29 months from the time I yielded to preach until the call came. I felt it breathing down my neck that whole time, yet I had no preconceived notion about how I would experience it. It was practically an electric jolt! God delights in the unexpected and cannot be scripted.

The third area, and the one that amused me for some years, is that I surrendered to go to Africa. But there was an era when everyone sincere Christian had to surrender to go to Africa. To my surprise I received an invitation to teach in Africa in 2003. I had no difficulty accepting the invitation, that had been decided over thirty years earlier! And I still teach in Africa although mostly through Zoom.

But I left the altar that August night confused. I did not receive any electrical jolt! But before I left the tabernacle I heard in my head, but not through my ears, "There is therefore now no condemnation." On my way to the bunk houses that Missouri sky looked brighter than it ever had. I woke the next more with a sense of God's presence I had never previously know. I even discovered that those words I heard were in the Bible — Romans 8:1.

When I returned home I told my parents I had gotten "sanctified." They said they thought I already was sanctified. My pastor must have thought the same thing because he had previously asked me to conduct a midweek service. But they did not know what was in my heart. I was defeated by sinful habits they knew nothing about. Had I not been delivered from the bondage of sin I would have crashed and burned years ago. I needed the inward power of the Holy Spirit.

After I was called to preach I turned to Romans 8 to preach sanctification because it talked so much about the Holy Spirit in that chapter. But as I went to a holiness Bible college I was finally required to read John Wesley. He described what had happened to me at camp, but he called it the new birth. I came to a crisis — would I preach my experience or would I preach biblically? I chose to preach biblically. As I studied Romans 8 I became convinced that it was describing regeneration, not a second blessing. And so I reinterpreted my experience to conform with that understanding. In the process my old friends and even my old church thought I had fallen into error — although they claimed to be "Wesleyan in doctrine."

Ken Collins wrote an article entitled, "Free!" In it he told of his discovery that faith in Christ had provided not only forgiveness of sins, but power over sin, the editor of the article inserted two sidebars on the doctrine of entire sanctification. Yet Collins told me he was not writing about his entire sanctification, but about his new birth.[240]

To this day I have never sought for nor received the gift of tongues. However, if the Lord gave it to me I would receive it. I have been heard and read in a multiplicity of languages, however. I am content to be a Bible Christian. I know I am accepted by God and walk in his presence. I don't where I fit, but I do know what I believe.

Wesley himself said, "My ground is the Bible. Yea, I am

---

[240]Collins, "Free!" 6-8.

a Bible-bigot. I follow it in all things, both great and small."[241] To those who claimed to have a better way, he demanded, "Show me it is so by plain proof of Scripture."[242]

It must have been the mercy of God that I did not receive an electrical jolt that August night in Missouri. Had I got what I expected I would have probably led people into error or started a new movement. It would have been shocking! I did not formulate a doctrinal paradigm to conform with my experience, but I sought to understand my personal experience in the light of biblical doctrine.

I have had some powerful encounters with God and I will take all such encounters as God wants me to have. Just one will cure a person of agnosticism! Yet I have never sought such encounters. I have walked with God most of my life and have enjoyed almost unbroken confidence and assurance of his acceptance since 1972.

Now much nearer the end than the beginning, some fifty plus years later, I seek to be made more like Christ. My greatest need is not to speak in tongues. Recently my neighbor chided me. He said that God would give tongues if I just asked him for it. But I don't want anything God does not want me to have. On an average day everyone I communicate with seems to understand English — except for the telemarketers who call incessantly! Furthermore, I don't need any language with which to communicate with God. He knows my very thoughts and we never stop sharing.

What I do need is more love, more patience and kindness. I seek for a daily delivery of God's love and I am sure those who live closest to me may even be praying more fervently

---

[241]Wesley, *Journal*, 5 June 1766.

[242]Wesley, *Preface* to Sermons, ¶ 9.

that this delivery is not delayed!

The Way Forward

The way forward is a return to seeking the Holy Spirit himself. We should seek the fruit of the Spirit and accept whatever gifts he bestows.

The twentieth-century Pentecostal movement was scorned by mainstream Christianity until it began to grow and they began to decline. Pragmatically, they then became willing to adopt and incorporate whatever would give them "success."

The chapter "Reconstructing a Spirit-led Movement," by Madeline Henners in *Reconstructing Methodism* represents John Wesley as a charismatic and advocates speaking in tongues. Henners quotes from Wesley's sermon, "The More Excellent Way." She quotes the second paragraph of this sermon, which makes Wesley sound charismatic. But in the very next paragraph he emphasizes the ordinary gifts as opposed to the extraordinary gift. For Wesley, the more excellent way was Christian perfection.[243]

Henners also quotes a statement from Rimi Xhemajli's book *The Supernatural and the Circuit Riders* (2021) that sounds in line with charismatic phenomena, but what this book demonstrates is that Methodism emphasized supernatural conversion. Yes, there were accounts of those who were slain in the Spirit. However, in the next paragraph Xhemajli concluded that supernatural manifestations were "orchestrated for a divine purpose: principally, to cause empirical demonstration of the existence of God and, ultimately, to make it possible for people to experience conversion." He also noted that Methodist circuit riders did not focus on speaking in

[243]Henners, *Reconstructing Methodism*, 55-76.

tongues.[244]

Speaking in tongues was not what caused the eighteen-century Methodist revival. Their emphasis was on ethical holiness which began at conversion. Their emphasis was on the fruit, not the gifts, of the Spirit.

> There is nothing higher in religion; there is, in effect, nothing else; if you look for anything but *more love*, you are looking wide of the mark, you are getting out of the royal way. And when you are asking others, "Have you received this or that blessing?" if you mean anything but *more love*, you mean wrong; you are leading them out of the way, and putting them upon a false scent. Settle it then in your heart, that from the moment God has saved you from all sin, you are to aim at nothing more, but more of that love described in the thirteenth of the Corinthians. You can go no higher than this, till you are carried into Abraham's bosom.[245]

---

[244]Xhemajli, *The Supernatural and the Circuit Riders*, 188, 261.

[245]Wesley, *BE Works*, 13:114.

BIBLIOGRAPHY

Anderson, Neil D. *A Definitive Study of Evidence concerning John Wesley's Appropriation of the Thought of Clement of Alexandria*. Lewiston, NY: Edwin Mellon Press, 2004.

Anderson, Robert Maples. *Vision of the Disinherited*. New York: Oxford University, 1979.

Arndt, William F. and F. Wilbur Gingrich. *A Greek-English Lexicon of the New Testament*. 2nd ed. Chicago: University of Chicago: 1979.

Bangs, Nathan. *The Necessity, Nature, and Fruits, of Sanctification: in a Series of Letters to a Friend*. 1851. Reprint, Salem, OH: Allegheny, 2006.

Barrett, David B, George Thomas Kurian, Todd M. Johnson, eds. *World Christian Encyclopedia*. 2nd ed. 2 vols. New York: Oxford University Press, 2001.

__________ and T. M. Johnson. "Global Statistics." *The New International Dictionary of Pentecostal and Charismatic Movements*, Stanley M. Burgess, ed, revised and expanded ed. Grand Rapids: Zondervan, 2002.

Behm, Johannes. γλῶσσα. *Theological Dictionary of the New Testament*. 10 vols. Gerhard Kittel and Gerhard Friedrich, eds. translated by Geoffrey W. Bromiley. Grand Rapids: Eerdmans, 1964. 1:722-724

Bennett, Dennis. *How to Pray for the Release of the Holy*

Spirit. South Plainfield, NJ: Logos, 1985.

__________."The Gifts of the Holy Spirit." *The Charismatic Movement*. Michael P. Hamilton, ed. Grand Rapids: Eerdmans, 1975.

Best, Ernest. *A Critical and Exegetical Commentary on - Ephesians: International Critical Commentary*. Edinburgh: T&T Clark, 1998. [*ICC*]

Black, David Alan. *Perspectives on the Ending of Mark: Four Views*. Nashville: B&H, 2008.

Blackwelder, Boyce. "The Glossolalia at Pentecost." *Vital Christianity* 83:10 (10 March 1963) 6.

Blaney, Harvey."St. Paul's Posture on Speaking in Unknown Tongues." *Wesleyan Theological Journal* 8:1 (Spring 1973) 52-60.

Bloesch, Donald G. *The Holy Spirit: Works and Gifts*. *Christian Foundations*. Downers Grove, IL: InterVarsity, 2000.

Burdick, Donald W. *Tongues: To Speak or Not to Speak*. Chicago: Moody, 1969.

Burgess, Stanley M. "The Ancient and Eastern Churches." and "The Medieval and Modern Western Churches." *Initial Evidence*. Gary B. McGee, ed. Peabody, MA: Hendrickson, 1991.

Carson, D. A. *Showing the Spirit: A Theological Exposition of 1 Corinthians 12-14*. Grand Rapids: Baker, 1987.

Carter, Charles W."A Wesleyan View of the Spirit's Gift of Tongues in the Book of Acts." *Wesleyan Theological Journal* 4:1 (Spring 1969) 39-68.

Cartwright, Peter. *Autobiography of Peter Cartwright*. 1856. Reprint, Nashville: Abingdon, 1984.

Chandler, Majorie Lee."Fuller Seminary Cancels Course on Signs and Wonders." *Christianity Today* 30:3 (21 Feb 1986) 48-49.

Christenson, Larry. *Answering Your Questions About Speaking in Tongues*. Minneapolis: Bethany House, 2005.

Clarke, Adam. *The Holy Bible, Containing the Old and New Testaments: The Text Carefully Printed from the Most Correct Copies of the Present Authorized Translations, Including the Marginal reading and Parallel Tests; with a Commentary and Critical Notes, Designed as a help to a Better Understanding of the Sacred Writings*. 6 vols. 1811-1825. Reprint, Nashville: Abingdon, 1950.

__________. *The Miscellaneous Works of Adam Clarke*. 13 vols. James Everett, ed. London: Thomas Tegg, 1836-1837.

__________. *The Miscellaneous Works of Adam Clarke*. 13 vols. James Everett, ed. London: T. Tegg, 1836-1837.

Collins, Kenneth J. "Free!" *Light and Life* (Jan 1986) 6-8.

Conn, Charles W. *Like a Mighty Army*. Cleveland, TN: Church of God, 1955.

Cox, Leo. *John Wesley's Concept of Perfection*. Kansas City: Beacon Hill, 1964.

Davidson, C. T. *Upon This Rock*. Cleveland, TN: White Wing, 1973.

Dallimore, Arnold A. *Forerunner of the Charismatic Movement: The Life of Edward Irving*. Chicago: Moody, 1983.

Dayton, Donald W. "The Doctrine of the Baptism of the Holy Spirit: Its Emergence and Significance."*Wesleyan Theological Journal* 13:1 (Spring 1978) 114-126.

Doty, Thomas K. *Lessons in Holiness*. 1881.Reprint, Salem, OH: Schmul, n. d.

Duewel, Wesley L. *The Holy Spirit and Tongues*. Winona Lake, IN: Light and Life, 1974.

Dunning, H. Ray. *Grace, Faith, and Holiness*. Kansas City: Beacon Hill, 1988.

Durham, William H. *Articles Written by Pastor W. H. Durham Taken From Pentecostal Testimony and Printed in Booklet Form*. n. p, n. d. The original articles were published between March 1909 - August 1912.

Edman, V. Raymond."Divine or Devilish." *Christian Herald* (May 1964) 14-17.

Farah, Charles. "America's Pentecostals: What They Believe." *Christianity Today* 31:15 (16 Oct 1987) 22-26.

Farrell, Frank. "Outburst of Tongues: The New Penetration." *Christianity Today* 7:24 (13 Sept 1963) 5.

Faupel, D. William."Glossolalia as Foreign Language: Investigation of the Early Twentieth-Century Pentecostal Claim." *Wesleyan Theological Journal* 31:1 (Spring 1996) 95-109.

Fletcher, John. *The Works of the Reverend John Fletcher*. 1833. Reprint, Salem, OH: Schmul, 1974.

Frame, John M. *The Doctrine of God*. Phillipsburg, NJ: Presbyterian & Reformed, 2002.

Garland, David E. *Baker Exegetical Commentary on the New Testament: 1 Corinthians*. Grand Rapids: Baker, 2003.

Garr, Alfred G. "A letter from Bro. Garr." *Confidence* 2 (May 1908) 21-22.

Gee, Donald. *Concerning Spiritual Gifts*. Springfield, MO: Gospel, 1972.

__________. *Speaking in Tongues: The Initial Evidence of the Baptism in the Holy Spirit*. Toronto: Full Gospel Publishing House, n. d.11 pages. Also printed by Gospel Publishing House in Springfield, MO as Tract #

951 and listed in their catalog as early as 1929-1930.Apparently this tract was also printed in Great Britain. See also *The Initial Evidence of the Baptism in the Holy Spirit*. Springfield, MO: Gospel Publishing House Tract #34-4677. 15 pages. This tract was later reprinted without Gee's name, perhaps in the 1980s. These tracts originated with his article "Speaking in Tongues, The Initial Evidence of the Baptism in the Holy Spirit." *Pentecostal Evangel* (12 December 1925) 6.

Godbey, William Baxter. *Church-Bride-Kingdom*. Cincinnati: Revivalist, 1905.

__________. *Spiritualism, Devil-worship and the Tongues*. Cincinnati: God's Revivalist, 1911.

__________. *Tongues Movement, Satanic*. Zarephath, NJ: Pillar of Fire, 1918.

__________. *Current Heresies*. Cincinnati: God's Revivalist, 1908.

__________. *Try the Spirits*. Greensboro, NC: Apostolic Messenger Office, 1909.

Goff, James M, Jr. *Fields White Unto Harvest: Charles F. Parham and the Missionary Origins of Pentecostalism*. Fayetteville, AR: University of Arkansas, 1988.

Goodman, Felicitas D. *Speaking in Tongues: A Cross-Cultural Study of Glossolalia*. Chicago: University of Chicago, 1972.

Goodwin, John. "Testing the Fruit of the Vineyard." http://www.biblebelievers.net/Charismatic/kjcviney.htm

Green, Roger J. *The Wesley Bible*. Albert F. Harper, ed. Nashville: Thomas Nelson, 1990.

Grudem, Wayne. *Systematic Theology*. Grand Rapids: Zondervan, 1994.

Gumbel, Nicky. *Telling Others: How to Run the Alpha Course*. London: Alpha, 2010.

Hall, J. L. "A Oneness Pentecostal Looks at Initial Evidence." *Initial Evidence*. Gary B. McGee, ed. Peabody, MA: Hendrickson, 1991.

Hanley, Irene. *Israel, O My People!* Decatur, GA: Vineyard Publishers of Atlanta, 1974.

Hart, Larry. "A Charismatic Perspective." *Perspectives on Spirit Baptism*. Chad Owen Brand, ed. Broadman & Holman, 2004.

Henners, Madeline C. "Reconstructing a Spirit-led Movement." Reconstructing Methodism: Crucial Issues Facing the Global Methodist Church, Matt O'Reilly, ed. Wilmore, KY: Francis Asbury Press, 2024.

Hills, A. M. *Holiness and Power*. 1897. Reprint, Noblesville, IN: Newby, n. d.

Hollenweger, Walter J. "Pentecostalism's Global Language: An Interview with Walter J. Hollenweger." *Christian History* 17:2 (Spring 1998) 42.

Horton, Stanley M. "The Pentecostal Perspective." *Five Views on Sanctification*. Grand Rapids: Zondervan, 1987.

__________. "Spirit Baptism: A Pentecostal Perspective." *Perspectives on Spirit Baptism*. Chad Owen Brand, ed. Broadman & Holman, 2004.

Hunt, John. *Letters on Entire Sanctification*. 1849. Reprint, Salem, OH: Schmul, 1984 as *Letters on Sanctification*.

Hurtado, Larry. "Normal, but Not a Norm: Initial Evidence and the New Testament." *Initial Evidence*. Gary B. McGee, ed. Peabody, MA: Hendrickson, 1991.

Irenaeus, *Against Heresies*. *The Ante-Nicene Fathers*. Vol. 1. Alexander Roberts and James Donaldson, eds. 1885. Reprint, Grand Rapids: Eerdmans, 1979. [*ANF*]

Isbell, Charles. "The Origins of Prophetic Frenzy and Ecstatic Utterance in the Old Testament World." *Wesleyan Theological Journal* 11:1 (Spring 1976) 62-80.

Jacobs, Mary. "Crash Course – Alpha courses offer basics of Christian faith." https://goodnewsmag.org/crash-course-alpha-courses-offer-basics-of-christian-faith/

Jennings, Daniel R. *The Supernatural Occurrences of John Wesley*. 2005. Reprinted, Sean Multimedia, 2012.

Jensen, Jerry, ed. *The Methodists and the Baptism of the Holy Spirit*. Los Angeles: Full Gospel Businessmen's Fellowship International, 1963.

Kantzer, Kenneth S. "The Charismatics Among Us." *Christianity Today* 24:4 (22 Feb 1980) 25.

Keen, S. A. *Salvation Papers*. Cincinnati: M. W. Knapp, 1896.

Keener, Craig S. *Acts: An Exegetical Commentary*. 4 vols. Grand Rapids: Baker, 2012.

Kelsey, Morton T. *Tongues Speaking*. Garden City, NY: Doubleday, 1968.

Kennedy, James H. *Early Days of Mormonism*. New York: Charles Scribner's Sons, 1888.

Kinghorn, Kenneth C. *Fresh Wind of the Spirit*. Nashville: Abingdon, 1975.

__________. *Gifts of the Spirit*. Nashville: Abingdon, 1976.

Kildahl, John. *The Psychology of Speaking in Tongues*. New York: Harper & Row, 1972.

Koch, Kurt E. *Occult ABC*. Grand Rapids: Kregel, 1978.

Kostlevy, William C. "Nor Silver, Nor Gold: The Burning Bush Movement and the Communitarian Holiness Vision." PhD diss, Notre Dame, 1996.

Krey, Philip D. W. and Peter D. S. Krey, eds. *Reformation Commentary on Scripture: Romans 9-16*. Vol. 8. Downers Grove, IL: InterVarsity, 2016 [*RCS*].

Koch, Kurt. *The Strife of Tongues*. Grand Rapids: Kregel, 1971.

Latourette, Kenneth Scott. *A History of Christianity*. 2 vols. 1975. Reprint, Peabody, MA: Prince, 1997.

Lewis, B. Scott. "William J. Seymour: Follower of the 'Eve ning Light.'" *Wesleyan Theological Journal* 39:2 (Fall 2004) 167-183.

Long, Elmer. *Recovering the Wesleyan Emphasis: The Life and Ministry of Elmer Long*. Vic Reasoner, ed. Evansville, IN: Fundamental Wesleyan, 2025.

Lowrey, Asbury. *Possibilities of Grace*. 1884. Reprint, Salem, OH: Allegheny, 1977.

MacArthur, John F. Jr. *Charismatic Chaos*. Grand Rapids: Zondervan, 1992.

__________. *The MacArthur New Testament Commentary on 1 Corinthians*. Chicago: Moody, 1984.

Maddox, Randy. *Responsible Grace*. Nashville: Abingdon, 1994.

Martin, Alfred. "Ephesians." *The Wycliffe Bible Commentary*. Everett F. Harrison, ed. Chicago: Moody, 1962.

Martin, Larry E. *The Life and Ministry of William J. Seymour*. Joplin, MO: Christian Life, 1999.

Maharaj, Rabindranth R. *Escape into the Light*. Eugene, OR: Harvest House, 1984.

Maloney, H. Newton and A. Adam Lovekin. *Glossolalia: Behavioral Science Perspectives on Speaking in Tongues*. New York: Oxford, 1985.

McCain, Danny. *Lord Lift Me Up!* Kuru, Nigeria: Reconnex Books, 2003.

__________. "The Baptism of the Holy Spirit." *The Arminian Magazine* 24:1 (Spring 2006) 1-5.

McCone, R. Clyde. *Culture and Controversy: An Investigation of the Tongues of Pentecost*. Philadelphia: Dorrance, 1978.

McGonigle, Herbert. "Pneumatological Nomenclature in Early Methodism." *Wesleyan Theological Journal* 8:1 (Spring 1973) 61-72.

McLaughlin, George A. *Commentary on the Acts of the Apostles*. 1915.Reprint, Salem, OH: Schmul, 1974.

McMullen, Cary."Holding Their Tongues." *Christianity Today* 53:10 (Oct 2009) 16.

Migne, Jacques Paul. *Patrologia Latina*. 1844-1845. 217 vols. Reprint, Alexandria, VA: Chadwyck-Healey, 1995.

Miley, John. *Systematic Theology*. 2 vols. 1893. Reprint, Peabody, MA: Hendrickson,1989.

Morris, Leon. *The Gospel According to John*. Rev. ed. *New International Commentary on the New Testament*. Grand Rapids: Eerdmans, 1995.

__________. *The Epistle to the Romans*: *The Pillar New Testament Commentary*, D. A. Carson, ed. Grand Rapids: Eerdmans, 1988.

O'Connor, Edward Dennis. *The Pentecostal Movement in the Catholic Church*. Notre Dame, IN: Ave Maria Press, 1971.

Oden, Thomas C. *Life in the Spirit: Systematic Theology: Volume Three*. San Francisco: HarperCollins, 1992.

Olsen, Ted. "What Really Unites Pentecostals?" *Christianity Today* 50:12 (Dec 2006) 18.

Oropeza, W. J. *A Time to Laugh: The Holy Laughter Phenomenon Examined — Guidelines for Distinguishing Genuine Renewal from Human-Induced Phenomena*.

Peabody, MA: Hendrickson, 1995.
Ozman, Agnes."When the Latter Rain First Fell: The First One to Speak in Tongues." *The Latter Rain Evangel* 1:4 (Jan 1919) 2.
Packer, J. I. "Charismatic Renewal: Pointing to a Person and a Power." *Christianity Today* 24:5 (7 March 1980) 16-17.
Patterson, Ben. "Cause for Concern." *Christianity Today* 30:11 (8 Aug 1986) 20.
Parham, Charles F. *The Sermons of Charles F. Parham: A Voice Crying in the Wilderness.* 1911. *The Everlasting Gospel.* 1944. Reprint, New York: Garland, 1985.
__________. "A Critical Analysis of the Tongues Question." *The Apostolic Faith* 25 (Baxter Springs) (June 1925) 2-6.
Parham, Sarah E. *The Life of Charles F. Parham: Founder of the Apostolic Faith Movement.* 1930. Reprint, New York: Garland, 1985.
Pattison, E. Mansell. "Speaking in Tongues and About Tongues." *Christian Standard* 98 (15 Feb 1964) 1-2.
Pawson, David. "A Mixed Blessing." *"Toronto" in Perspective: Papers on the New Charismatic Wave of the mid-1900s.* David Hilborn, ed. Carlisle, Cumbria, Great Britain: Paternoster, 2001.
Percy, Martyn. *Words, Wonders and Power.* London: SPCK, 1996.
Pinnock, Clark H. *An Evangelical Theology of the Charismatic Renewal.* Vancouver: Clark H. Pinnock, 1975. Nine pages, apparently an address given at Regent College in May 1975.
__________. "Tongues." *A Theological Evaluation and Critique.* Luther B. Dyer, ed. Jefferson City, MO: LeRoi, 1971.

__________ and Grant R. Osborne. "A Truce Proposal for the Tongues Controversy." *Christianity Today* 16:1 (8 Oct 1971) 6-9.

__________. *Flame of Love*. Downers Grove, IL: InterVarsity, 1996.

__________. "Evangelical Theologians Facing the Future: Ancient and Future Paradigms." *Wesleyan Theological Journal* 33:2 (Fall 1998) 7-28.

Platt, Frederic. "Perfection (Christian)." *Encyclopedia of Religion and Ethics*.12 vols. James Hastings, ed. Edinburgh: T. & T. Clark, 1908-1927.

Poole, William Henry. *Ripe Grapes: The Fruit of the Spirit*. 1881. Reprint, Salem, OH: Schmul, 1999.

Pope, William Burt. *A Compendium of Christian Theology*. 3 vols. London: Wesleyan Conference Office, 1880.

Purkiser, W. T. *The Gifts of the Spirit*. Kansas City: Beacon Hill, 1975.

Quebedeaux, Richard. *The New Charismatics*. Garden City, NY: Doubleday, 1976.

"A Queer Faith." *Topeka Daily Capital* (6 January 1901) 2.

Reasoner, Vic. *A Wesleyan Theology of Holy Living for the Twenty-First Century*. 2 vols. Evansville, IN: Fundamental Wesleyan, 2012.

__________. "Review." *The Arminian Magazine*. 24:1 (Spring 2006) 11-12.

Ridgway, James H. "Psychology: Theology of the Human Psyche." *A Contemporary Wesleyan Theology*. 2 vols. Charles W. Carter, ed. Grand Rapids: Francis Asbury, 1983.

Robeck, Cecil M, Jr. *The Azusa Street Mission and Revival*. Nashville: Thomas Nelson, 2006.

__________. "William J. Seymour and 'the Bible Evidence.'" *Initial Evidence*. Gary B. McGee, ed. Peabody, MA: Hendrickson, 1991.

Roberts, Oral. *The Baptism with the Holy Spirit and the Value of Speaking in Tongues Today*. Tulsa, OK: Published by the author, 1964.

__________. *The Holy Spirit and the Now I*. Tulsa, OK: Oral Roberts University, 1974.

Sangster, W. E. *The Pure in Heart*. 1954. Reprint, Salem, OH: Schmul, 1984.

Schwab, Matthew and Kathleen. *Speaking in Tongues: Enjoying Intimacy With God Through Tongues and Interpretation*. Called Writers Christian Publishers, 2020.

Schwartz, Hillel. *The French Prophets*. Berkeley: University of California, 1980.

Seebass, Horst. "Holy." *The New International Dictionary of New Testament Theology*. 3 vols. Colin Brown, ed. Grand Rapids: Zondervan, 1976.

Seymour, W. J. *The Doctrines and Disciplines of the Azusa Street Apostolic Faith Mission of Los Angeles, California*. Los Angeles: W. J. Seymour, 1915.

Shumway, Charles William. "A Study of 'The Gift of Tongues.'" A. B. thesis, University of Southern California, 1914.

__________. "A Critical History of Glossolalia." PhD diss, Boston University, 1919.

Smith, George. *Elements of Divinity*. Nashville: Southern Methodist Publishing House, 1860.

Smith, Joseph. *History of the Church of Jesus Christ of Latter-Day Saints*. 6th ed. 7 vols. Salt Lake City: Deseret, 1960.

Smith, Larry D. *A Century on the Mount of Blessings: The Story of God's Bible School*. Cincinnati: Revivalist Press, 2016.

Snyder, Howard A. "The Church as Holy and Charismatic."

Wesleyan Theological Journal 15:2 (Fall 1980) 7-32.

__________ with Daniel V. Runyon. *The Divided Flame: Wesleyans and the Charismatic Renewal.* Grand Rapids: Francis Asbury, 1986.

Spittler, Russell."The Pentecostal Tradition, Part IV." *Agora* 2:3 (Spring 1979) 4.

Stafford, Tim. "The Pentecostal Gold Standard." *Christianity Today* 49:7 (July 2005) 28.

__________. "Testing the Wine from John Wimber's Vineyard." *Christianity Today* 30:11 (8 Aug 1986) 17-22.

Stagg, Frank, E. Glenn Hinson, and Wayne E. Oates. *Glossolalia*. Nashville: Abingdon, 1967.

Staples, Rob L. *Outward Sign and Inward Grace*. Kansas City: Beacon Hill, 1991.

__________. "A Rose is a Rose is (Not Always) a Rose." *Holiness Today* 1:10 (Oct 1999) 25.

Steadman, J. M. "The Gift of Tongues and Kindred Phenomena." *Methodist Quarterly Review* 74 (Oct 1925) 688-715.

Steele, Daniel. *The Gospel of the Comforter*. 1897. Reprinted, Salem, OH: H. E. Schmul, 1973.

Storm, C. Samuel. "A Third Wave View." *Are Miraculous Gifts for Today? Four Views*. Wayne A. Grudem, ed. Grand Rapids: Zondervan, 1996.

__________. *The Language of Heaven*. Lake Mary, FL: Charisma House, 2019.

Stott, John R. W. *The Message of Romans: God's Good News for the World*. Downers Grove, IL: InterVarsity, 1994.

Summers, Thomas O. *Holiness: A Treatise on Sanctification, as Set Forth in the New Testament*. 1851. Reprint, Louisville, KY: Pentecostal Publishing,1897.

Swaggart, Jimmy. *Is Speaking in Tongues Scriptural and*

Relevant to This Day and Age? Baton Rouge, LA: Jimmy Swaggart Ministries, 1982.
Synan, Vinson. *The Holiness-Pentecostal Tradition: Charismatic Movements in the Twentieth Century*. Grand Rapids: Eerdmans, 1997.
__________. "Introduction." to Frank Bartleman. *Azusa Street*. Plainfield, NJ: Logos, 1980.
__________ and Daniel Woods. *Fire Baptized: The Many Lives and Works of Benjamin Hardin Irwin: A Biography and a Reader*. Lexington, KY: Emeth, 2017.
Taylor, George. *The Spirit and the Bride: A Scriptural Presentation of the Operations, Manifestations, Gifts and Fruit of the Holy Spirit in Relation to His Bride with Special Reference to the Latter Rain Revival*. Dunn, NC: published by the author, 1907.
Tertullian, *The Prescription Against Heretics. The Ante-Nicene Fathers*. Vol. 3. Alexander Roberts and James Donaldson, eds. 1885. Reprint, Grand Rapids: Eerdmans, 1978. [*ANF*]
Thayer, Joseph Henry. *Greek English Lexicon of the New Testament*. 1885. Reprint, Grand Rapids: Zondervan, 1981.
Todd, S. C. "Some Sad Failures of Tongues in Mission Fields." *Baptist Argus* 12:4 (Louisville, KY), (23 Jan 1908) 1-2.
__________. "An Open Letter: Being a calm review of the Speaking in Tongues in South China." Macao, China: Bible Missionary Society, 1908.
Turner, George Allen. *The Evangelical Commentary: The Gospel According to John*. Grand Rapids: Eerdmans, 1964.
Tuttle, Robert G. Jr. *Guidelines: The United Methodist Church and the Charismatic Movement*. Nashville:

Discipleship Resources, 1976.
Wacker, Grant. "Wimber and Wonders — What about Miracles Today?" *The Reformed Theological Journal* 37:4 (April 1987) 16-19.
__________. *Heaven Below: Early Pentecostals and American Culture*. Cambridge, MA: Harvard University Press, 2001.
Wagner, C. Peter. "MC510: Signs, Wonders and Church Growth." *Christian Life* 44:6 (Oct 1982) 42-49.
__________. *Acts of the Holy Spirit*. Ventura, CA: Regal, 2000.
Wallace, Daniel B. *Greek Grammar: Beyond the Basics*. Grand Rapids: Zondervan, 1996.
Walvoord, John F. *The Holy Spirit*. 3rd ed. Grand Rapids: Zondervan, 1958.
__________. "The Augustinian -Dispensational Perspective." *Five Views on Sanctification*. Grand Rapids: Zondervan, 1987.
Watson, George D. *The Bridehood Saints*. Cincinnati: God's Revivalist, 1913.
Wesley, Charles. *The Journal of the Rev. Charles Wesley, M. A.* Thomas Jackson, ed. 2 vols. 1849. Reprint, Grand Rapids: Baker, 1980.
Wesley, John. *The Bicentennial Edition of the Works of John Wesley*. Randy Maddox, ed. 35 vols when complete. Nashville: Abingdon, 1976-.
__________, *Explanatory Notes Upon the New Testament*. 1754. Reprint, Schmul, 1976.
White, Alma. *Demons and Tongues*. Zarephath, NJ: Pillar of Fire, 1936.
Williams, J. Rodman. "Charismatic Movement." *Evangelical Dictionary of Theology*. Walter A. Elwell, ed. Grand Rapids: Baker, 1996.

Wilson, W. C. *Well Glory!* mss; Church of the Nazarene Archives, Kansas City, MO.

Wimber, John. *Power Points*. San Francisco: HarperCollins, 1991.

Witherington, Ben. *The Acts of the Apostles: A Socio-Rhetorical Commentary*. Grand Rapids: Eerdmans, 1998.

Wood, Laurence W. *Pentecostal Grace*. Wilmore, KY: Francis Asbury, 1980.

__________. *The Meaning of Pentecost in Early Methodism*. Landham, MD: Scarecrow, 2002.

Xhemajli, Rimi. *The Supernatural and the Circuit Riders*. Eugene, OR: Pickwick, 2021.

Yocum, Dale M. *Conformed to Christ*. Cincinnati: Revivalist, 1962.

__________. "Five-year-old Victor Walks Again." *The Wesleyan Methodist* 119:44 (1 November 1961) 9.